Series/Number 06-005

Patterns of Social and Political Mobilization:
A Historical Analysis of the
Nordic Countries

STEIN KUHNLE
Institute of Sociology
University of Bergen

 SAGE Publications/London/Beverly Hills

For information address

SAGE PUBLICATIONS, Ltd.,
St. George's House/44 Hatton Garden
London EC1N 8ER

SAGE PUBLICATIONS, INC.
275 South Beverly Drive
Beverly Hills, California 90212

International Standard Book Number 0-8039-9908-9

Library of Congress Catalogue Card No. L.C. 74-84259

FIRST PRINTING

Printed by Wells & Blackwell Ltd., Churchgate, Loughborough, Leics.

CONTENTS

ACKNOWLEDGEMENTS

This report is part of a cross-national study of nationbuilding in Europe, directed by Stein Rokkan. The project has been supported by a grant from the Norwegian Research Council (*NAVF*).

The study arose from discussions with Stein Rokkan and Frank H. Aarebrot, and was further stimulated by earlier work in the field of social and political mobilization by Rokkan, William Lafferty, Wolfgang Zapf and Peter Flora.

Stein Rokkan and Derek Urwin have spent a considerable amount of time commenting in depth upon earlier drafts, and to them I owe a special debt of gratitude. I would also like to thank Frank Aarebrot, Gudmund Hernes, Lars Svåsand and Helge Østbye who have commented upon various parts of the study. I am much obliged to Derek Urwin who offered advice on the quality and style of my English prose.

Patterns of Social and Political Mobilization: A Historical Analysis of the Nordic Countries

STEIN KUHNLE

I. THEME OF STUDY

The phenomenon to be studied is political participation. The initial question is simple: what socio-economic circumstances make for higher or lower levels of political participation in a polity and what are the preconditions for a politically "mobilized" society? A study of this kind can be performed on different societal levels: nation, region, commune, individual. Hence they will differ from each other in their degree of detail, for example in the number of independent and dependent variables included and controlled for.

The analysis here consists of a comparative macro study of relationships between social and economic change, political incorporation,[1] and political participation. Its empirical basis is time-series data for four Nordic countries: Denmark, Finland, Norway and Sweden.[2] The units of analysis will in most cases be nations and in some cases also geographical regions and provinces within nations. In this first round, we are primarily interested in obtaining an overall impression of differences at macro levels. Partly because of the workload involved in data collection, we shall confine ourselves to a few, rather straightforward, variables. We have selected some of the most common indicators of social mobilization used.[3] The indicator of level of political participation will be voting turnout in national elections. We shall go as far back in time as the availability of data on turnout permits.

All four countries have developed into modern welfare societies, and share many traits. Without providing data here it can be stated in general

NOTE: All data used in this study are documented in: Stein Kuhnle, "Social mobilization and political participation: the Nordic countries c.1850-1970," Institute of Sociology, University of Bergen, Autumn 1973 (mimeo).

terms that the population sizes, levels of economic development, social structures, political ideologies, party systems, international status, and except for Denmark, extent of geographical area are all quite similar. The intention here is to describe empirically the different paths followed by these four countries towards their present socio-political state.

The historical preconditions differed somewhat in the four countries. Obviously, we shall have to include *system-specific variables to account for differences in response* of élites to suffrage extensions and of masses to new opportunities. The argument shall be that the analysis of *specific* political contexts is relevant for an understanding of *initial* levels of political mobilization, and that the analysis of *general* processes of social mobilization may shed light upon the *trends* of political mobilization. The design can be expressed in the terms of a regression equation where x would be time and where political *context* would account for the difference in the a (= the initial level of political mobilization) and where social mobilization could account for the difference in the b (= the slope).

The study seeks answers to several questions. What are the consequences of the fact that larger and larger proportions of the population move to, and settle down in towns? What are the political consequences of increased economic productivity and a general and gradual increase in the level of social welfare? What does the mobilization within the labour force sector imply: the fact that people break away from small, agricultural communities and move in to industrial and "tertiary" work? What are the political effects of the spread of education and the advance of literary and technical skills? We shall make use of the concept "social mobilization" to characterize these processes of change. This concept was first developed by Deutsch (1961: 493) for whom "social mobilization is a name given to an overall process of change, which happens to substantial parts of the population in countries which are moving from traditional to modern ways of life". Social mobilization appears "over a longer period as one of its [modernization's] continuing aspects and as a significant cause, in the well-known pattern of feedback or circular causation". He then proceeds by listing the quantitative characteristics of countries undergoing rapid social mobilization: for example, the average annual increase in literacy, population growth, mass media audience, voting participation, occupational shift out of agriculture, income growth, specifying in each case growth rates in percentages. Deutsch's concept is very comprehensive, and only some of the dimensions have been singled out. [4] Moreover, we have chosen to regard one of the phenomena – voting participation – as dependent upon the others. This way of interpreting interrelationships between socio-economic change and political development is far from original, and was suggested by Deutsch himself: "Where people have the right to vote, the effects of social mobilization are likely to be reflected in the electoral statistics. This process finds its expression both through a tendency towards a higher voting participation of those already enfranchised and through an extension of the franchise itself to additional groups of the population" (Deutsch, 1961: 500).

In essence, the focus of this work is to study the degree to which it holds true that social mobilization is followed or accompanied by an increase in political participation. The study is organized in three major parts:

1. History; what is the impact of state-building on initial political mobilization? What are the consequences of the history of representative organs? What are the immediate effects of establishment of mass parties? What are the patterns of political mobilization when controlled for "political time periods"?

2. Concepts; this part discusses political mobilization as a process of diffusion of participation norms, and discusses the selection and interpretation of indicators of social mobilization.

3. Analysis; what are the effects of levels and tempo of social mobilization on political mobilization? To what extent is level of political mobilization dependent upon geographical-political location? What are the differences between "centre" and "periphery"?

II. HISTORICAL BACKGROUND

Introduction

Four aspects of historical-political development will be touched upon. They are all assumed to be specifically relevant to the study of political mobilization:

1. the *foundation* or formation of the nation-state; the history of dependence and independence; in which geopolitical context have the countries been located?

2. the development of *representative* organs; the existence and timing of different institutions;

3. the *incorporation* of citizens into the political system; who has had the opportunity to participate?

4. the development of *political infrastructure;* political parties; when were organized channels of interest and demand articulation established?

On each of these subjects we shall try to outline the main facts of history,[5] and add personal speculations as to possible consequences for the start level of political mobilization. We shall in this section relate political participation trends to more strictly *political* events and political developmental traits. The data handled in this section are of a more qualitative nature (e.g., presence/absence of a suffrage qualification), but some may also be understood in quantitative terms (e.g., the *timing* of an introduction of new suffrage rules, and the *porportions* of people qualified).

State Formation

All four countries have formed, or been members of, medieval dynasties, by contrast to territories that have been, or been parts of, continental empires.

Denmark and Sweden may be classified as "older" nation-states in terms of their history of national independence. Both were unified before the 10th century A.D. Finland must be characterized as a newer state. No independent state formation existed before Sweden expanded its boundaries eastwards in the 12-13th centuries. Finland became a part of Sweden until 1809, when it became a province of Russia, a "partnership" Finland managed to secede from in 1917. Norway may also be labelled a newer secession state, though it obviously was an independent state formation from its unification in about A.D. 900 until Denmark vassalized the country in 1380. Norway remained a province of Denmark for 430 years. In 1814 it had to enter, as a result of the peace agreement in Kiel, a "personal union" with Sweden instead; a loose federation, though frequently a very hot issue in Norwegian debate, that lasted until 1905.

The concepts of "dependent" and "independent" are broad and discrete. We should ask: What *aspects* of social life — economy, culture, politics — were influenced? What *degree* of dependence? How strict were the administrative/governmental regulations in different fields? These questions make it possible to differentiate the concept "dependence" in the case of Norway and Finland, and also differentiate time periods. A third question, which would demand an analysis of its own to answer, could be: dependence for *whom*? In other words, which population groups were concerned, certain élite groupings only, or the "masses"? This question is related not only to the build-up of domestic political institutions and degree of democracy, but also to the level of social mobilization, i.e., the information level of the population and the awareness of political input and output processes.

Nationalist emotions were generated earlier in Norway than in Finland. This could be ascribed to the fact that Finland had not achieved status as an independent state until Sweden colonized the area. Norway was integrated earlier, and had experienced sovereignty. The Norwegian dependence upon Denmark was by and large strict, especially during the period of absolutism from 1660 onwards: Copenhagen was the selected capital of the two countries, with strong centralization of all power by the king in Copenhagen, and a common government for the two countries (the Danish government had governed Norway from 1537). In addition there was a high justice of court, and a common university, both situated in Copenhagen. The king appointed all governmental officials, clergymen, city-mayors and city-councils. *Fogder* were sent around to collect taxes and the money was transferred directly to the central government in Copenhagen. Under the early Danish period in Norway, foreign noblemen were appointed *lensherrer,* and the Church was dominated by Danes, bishops being appointed from Denmark. The Norwegian "national" income was mainly used for Danish purposes. The Danish language gained a strong foothold in the Norwegian bureaucracy during this early Danish period, and became a cultural influence of great importance when the school system was built up from the 1740s. In sum, Denmark had a strong grip on most spheres of life in politics, economy and culture.

By contrast, the 90-year union with Sweden was loose, and Norway enjoyed almost complete domestic self-government, although several clashes occurred between the Swedish King and the Norwegian Parliament and bureaucracy. The only restricted field was foreign policy. The union was dissolved (by Norway!) in 1905 on the question of an independent Norwegian department for foreign affairs and diplomatic relations. During the whole period of the union, Sweden, in contrast to Denmark earlier, made no attempts at directing and controlling economic and cultural life. In fact, Norway's "protected" role internationally may have been very advantageous for domestic development.

Before 1809, Finland's history was equivalent to the history of Sweden: that is, Sweden had almost complete control of all policy and administrative questions. Finland was a part of the Swedish state that functioned as any other administrative part of Sweden although some Finns also had limited influence in Sweden. Finland's status of dependence was not changed very much as a Grand Duchy of Russia after 1809. The

Church operated as before, and Finland maintained Swedish law. However, the bureaucracy was adjusted to the Russian pattern. The period 1809-1863 was in fact a period of absolutism: no parliament (the Diet of the four estates) was assembled.

From the 1860s, national sentiments started to rise. This could be taken as a sign of increasing social mobilization. A kind of nationalistic movement began among academicians in Åbo, and both Swedish and Russian influence in Finnish society was attacked. It was a political as well as a cultural awakening: the goal was an independent nation-state with Finnish as the only language to be taught in school and to be used in the bureaucracy. Another movement based upon the Swedish population set aside the language question as less important, but stressed the demand for a *politically* independent Finland. Political life was democratized from 1863, and the *Lantdag* was assembled nine times until 1894, when the czar, Nikolai II, started a severe "russification" (the wave of national sentiments had reached and swept across Russia too!). The Finns were forced to accept several curtailments of the provisions in their constitution of 1809: Finnish soldiers were to be trained in Russian troops (1898); Russian was introduced as the official language of the bureaucracy (1900); and Russians were granted governmental positions in Finland (1902). Finnish opposition was obstructed by press censorship, and the rights of organization and assembly were restricted. In fact, a new period of absolutism was introduced from 1899 onwards. Under the pressure of revolutionary groups inside Russia, the defeats in the fight against Japan, and the "Big Strike" in Finland in 1905, the czar and the Russian government were forced to accept Finnish proposals for a reorganization of the parliament. Social life in Finland was highly politicized in this period from 1894 until 1906, and the (severe) presence of a foreign enemy helps explain the extraordinary mobilization of the Finnish electorate in the first election under new rules with universal suffrage, when turnout was 70 per cent. Finland had to endure another 11 years under Russia: the First World War and the Russian Revolution made a successful secession possible.

In both Finland and Norway one should expect higher mobilization rates after enfranchisement than in Denmark and Sweden. The presence of a foreign enemy planted inside the two countries is assumed to make for a greater awareness of political problems, and to help to unite and mobilize *all* population groups.

Organs of Representation

Sweden has had the most continuous institution of representation of the four countries. Though Sweden had a king, it was organized in a decentralized manner in the medieval period: different parts of the country enjoyed extensive autonomy. The country has had a very long tradition of representative organs, and the power of the king was limited at an early stage. The *Riksdag*, the assembly of the four estates of Nobles, Clergymen, Burghers and Farmers, became firmly organized from about 1600 onwards. The period from 1680 to 1719 was in reality dominated by an absolutist king, but it was followed bv a 50 year period ("The Era of Liberty") when the *Riksdag* monopolized governmental power. The king regained complete hegemony for a 40-year period until 1809 when he was overthrown in a *coup d'état*. Another attempt was then made to establish balanced relationships between the highest executive and the representative organ of the people.

The undemocratic institution of the estate assembly was abolished first in 1866. A new Parliament Act established a bicameral structure, each chamber possessing equal competence and authority. The First Chamber was given the character of an upper house; elections were indirect through country and city-councils, and members were elected for nine-year periods. Rules of eligibility were strict, but the primary electorate was probably larger than the electorate for the Second Chamber, elections to which could be either direct or indirect. It was direct in towns, but left to the discretion of local authorities in rural areas. The suffrage for the Second Chamber was even more limited than the Norwegian rules of 1814! The Upper House was abolished in 1970 and replaced by a unicameral parliament.

In the Middle Ages, an institution called the *Danehoff* existed as a kind of government in Denmark. It was composed of noblemen, representatives of the Church, and representatives of so called "public interests". The *Danehoff* met yearly after 1282. In 1400, an aristocratic council replaced the *Danehoff* and in 1660 the king introduced absolutism, concentrating executive, legislative and judiciary powers in his own hands. Absolutist rule by the king prevailed undisturbed until 1830, when the Danish population was also affected by the July revolution. The king was pressed to introduce and accept an "estate constitution" in 1834. Four regional, advisory estate assemblies — but no new central authority — were established. The electorate — consisting of farm-owners, leaseholders with large farms, and property-owning burghers in the towns — voted within three classes, but the elected representatives assembled in a one-chamber institution. The separation into four different assemblies made a corporate, powerful opposition difficult.

In the middle of the war between Denmark and Prussia, the National-Liberals paved the way for a new constitution, signed by the king in June 1849. It represented a drastic jump on the way to popular democracy, with widespread enfranchisement. Denmark obtained a two-chamber parliament: the *Folketing* (the Lower House) and the *Landsting* (the Upper House). This organization lasted until the constitution of 1953, when the Upper House was disbanded. Elections for the Lower House were direct, while indirect elections with very restrictive suffrage rules prevailed for the selection of Upper House representatives. A revision of the constitution in 1866 moved *Landstinget* into an even more conservative position, in that 15 per cent of the representatives were to be appointed by the king. *Landstinget* was democratized in 1915, when universal suffrage was introduced for both chambers, but the minimum voting age was set at 35. Since 1915, proposals for constitutional changes have had to be accepted through general referenda.

Before 1809, Finland's constitutional history equalled that of Sweden. When Russia replaced Sweden as the "imperial" power, Finland maintained its "Gustavian" constitution of 1772 and 1789: that is, the four estates of the Nobility, Clergy, Burgesses and Peasants continued to elect representatives to a four-chamber legislature. But the czar possessed the final authority: he did not assemble the parliament until 1863. This was possible because the constitution contained no provisions on how frequent the estates should be summoned. The Diet of the four estates decided on a new Parliament Act in 1906, and strangely enough, the estates replaced themselves with a unicameral *eduskunta* in 1907. A proportional system of representation was adopted, and universal suffrage introduced.

The Norwegian constitution dates from 1814, when the country enjoyed a brief period as an independent nation until Sweden replaced Denmark as master of the house. This constitution was respected by the Swedish king, and it represented a considerable impetus towards democracy: from 150 years under absolutist rule by the Danish king to domestic independence with liberal suffrage qualifications – in fact the most liberal in Europe at that time. However, elections remained indirect until 1906. The Norwegian *Storting* is basically unicameral, but is divided into two chambers for the handling of law proposals. But Norway rejected the idea of an upper house composed of partly elected, partly appointed, "privileged" people (Norway was also the first of the Nordic countries to abolish the institution of the Nobility in 1821). Norway led the way for democratization in the Nordic context, and served as an example, attractive and/or appalling, in the discussion of parliamentary reform in the Swedish *Riksdag* in the 1830s and 40s. However, Sweden retained the estate-assembly until 1866. In 1884 the Norwegian *Storting* became the first Nordic parliament to enforce the principle of parliamentarism. The issue of parliamentarism was brought to the fore in Denmark in the 1870s, but the principle was not accepted until 1901, when the king simply could not disregard a liberal majority of 85 out of 114 *Folketing*-representatives! Sweden adopted the parliamentarian principle as late as 1917, while in Finland it was introduced through a Government Act in 1919, in connection with the secession from Russia (or Soviet).

The election procedures for these representative organs can also be measured and weighed on a dimension of "democraticness".[6] The more direct the elections, the more democratic, and the more mathematically proportional (in relation to parties) the representation, the more democratic the institution. Accepting the above evaluations, and the additional points that secret voting is more democratic than open voting, and that the principle of one-man, one-vote is more democratic than plural voting, one can conclude that Norway possessed the most democratic representative institution in the last century (also taking into consideration the absence of a powerful upper house, but here disregarding level/degree of enfranchisement), and that Finland was the first country to introduce a completely democratic institution. The history of representation is also assumed to have effects on the level and tempo of political mobilization. In a system with a long continuity of representative organs, combined with a long history of independence, a *gradual* increase in political participation may be expected. People in general are supposed not to be as "politicized" as in countries having experienced colonization. Political leaders have not had to mobilize the people against any common enemy, while most leaders in "occupied" countries are supposed to make persistent attempts to rally the support of the whole population in efforts to eject uninvited visitors from the country. Leaving aside social mobilization, the argument would look like this:

	Continuous organs of representation:	Protracted absolutist rule:
"Old" independent nations	(1) gradual, late political mobilization	(2) mobilization earlier than in (1)
"Newer" secession states	(3) early mobilization higher participation rates than in (1) and (2)	(4) early, relatively (to (1), (2), (3)) high mobilization

As is seen, both the history of independence and the history of the representative organs are suggested to be variables capable of explaining some of the differences in the initial mobilization rates: political mobilization being higher in newer secession states than in old, independent ones, and also higher in systems with protracted absolutist rule than in systems with continuous organs of representation. However, the first factor is assumed to carry more weight. Since the populations of old-established, independent nations are assumed to be less mobilized for external purposes, they are assumed to be less mobilized in general.

A further related proposition would be that democratization in terms of organs of representation and voting right would occur earlier in cells (2) and (4) than in cells (1) and (3). Greater proportions of the populations are supposed to be "suffering", or to have a feeling of injustice, in a system with absolutist rule, thereby creating a more wide-spread demand for democratization: e.g., Denmark may be contrasted to Sweden, and Norway to Sweden. Elite groupings that have themselves been denied the right and opportunity to govern will not have the same fears of steps towards democratization. Both the demand for participation rights and actual participation are expected to be higher in cases (2) and (4) than in the others. The four Nordic countries are located as such in the above table: (1) Sweden; (2) Denmark; (3) Finland; (4) Norway.

These propositions will be discussed through confrontation with empirical data in the section to follow. However, there are too few cases to test the general validity of them, and for example it is difficult to find instruments to measure in any strict way *demand* for democratization.

The Effect of the Institutional Heritage on Initial Mobilization Levels

Figure 1 compares the empirical curves of political mobilization in the four countries. It represents a "test" of the propositions set forth at the end of the previous section. The following conclusions are suggested:

1. As expected, the Figure demonstrates that Sweden experienced a political mobilization process *later* than the other countries, and the mobilization may possibly be said to have been more gradual and even. Electoral turnout was higher in Norway in the period 1829-1868, than in Sweden in the 1870s. One notices also that Denmark mobilized earlier than Sweden, and that participation rates were never as low in Norway as in Denmark in their early electoral history. These results seem to correspond to the predictions.

2. We observe very similar participation trends in Denmark, Norway and Sweden in the period 1868-1908. The curves have the same shapes, but the *timing* of mobilization is conspicuous: Denmark first, Norway

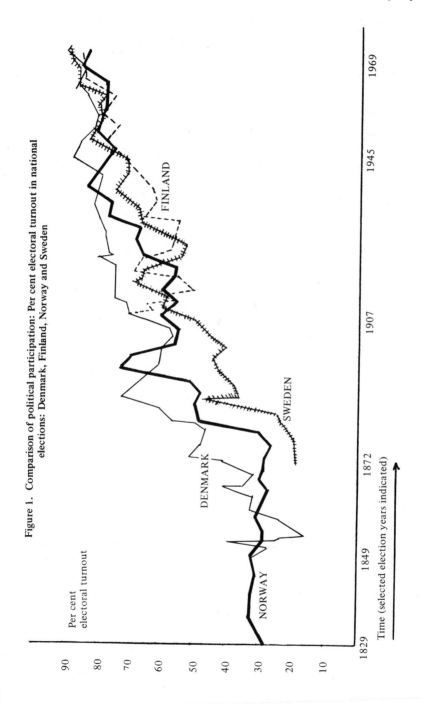

Figure 1. Comparison of political participation: Per cent electoral turnout in national elections: Denmark, Finland, Norway and Sweden

Per cent electoral turnout

FINLAND

DENMARK

SWEDEN

NORWAY

Time (selected election years indicated)

1829   1849   1872   1907   1945   1969

90 80 70 60 50 40 30 20 10

second, Sweden third. This is a time period during which the immediate effects of statebuilding and history of representative organs in Denmark and Norway should have disappeared, and we may expect social forces in general to play a more vital mobilizing role (compare with test of hypothesis 1 in section IV, where data on social mobilization are provided).

3. Finland experienced a "participation shock" in its first election with universal suffrage in 1907. The impact of the Russian colonial power on social and political life must have been enormous. Participation dropped gradually, but reached another peak in 1917, when Finland succeeded in freeing itself from Russia. After independence, participation declined again and the trend turned more "normal" — participation rates lagging behind the other Nordic countries until the 1950s and 60s. Early mobilization in Finland must be understood in terms of extraordinary political events — and the lag in the Nordic context after independence may possibly be accounted for by the relatively late social mobilization (cf. Section IV).

4. The fact that the mobilization curves of Denmark, Norway and Sweden have approximately the same shapes, while the curve of Finland has a somewhat different shape (the initial part of the curve), suggests that even though Denmark, Norway and Sweden have had different developments of statebuilding and representative organs, their historical developments are more comparable than any of the three developments with Finland's. When we compare the historical development of Finland and Norway, it is probably a very important factor that Norway reached near-independence 100 years earlier than Finland. The *timing* of independence occurred at different stages of social and cultural mobilization in the two countries — thus assigning the status of being an oppressed colony under Russia a much greater weight than the change from (Danish) absolutist rule to constitutional organs of representation in Norway in explaining differences in initial political mobilization.

Thresholds of Incorporation

Norway was the first of the Nordic countries to carry through a major democratization of political rights. After 150 years of absolutist rule by the Danish king, the Norwegians saw a chance of becoming independent with a king of its own when Denmark was defeated during the Napoleonic wars. A constitution was written, and though the suffrage rules finally agreed upon must have been considered very radical at that time, even more radical proposals were set forth, but voted down. The constitution was respected by Sweden, when Norway was forced to join a so-called personal union with Sweden, as a result of the Napoleonic war-outcome, in

1814-15.

All independent farmers, and peasants who had leased a farm for at least five years, were given the right to vote. In the towns burghers, higher state officials and people who owned a house or property were qualified to vote. The rights of women were not mentioned in the constitution: obviously it was not even seen necessary to state formally that women were denied participation rights. Altogether about 45 per cent of all men above the age of 25 were given the right to vote, thus introducing the most democratic suffrage system in Europe at that time (Kuhnle, 1972). However, those qualified had to register, thus demanding a "two-stage" initiative from potential voters. In addition, elections were made indirect — another way of restricting in practice the otherwise liberal suffrage. The proportion of men above 25 years of age qualified to vote decreased over time, due to the fact that the rules favoured the farm-population, and the decrease of the proportion of farmers in the total male population.

Denmark was the country that followed the Norwegian path most closely. The absolutist rule was gradually coming to an end, Danish élite-groups being able to push through representation of estates in the wake of the July revolution. During the war between Denmark and Prussia in 1849, King Frederick VII signed a new constitution which represented a major step towards democratic participation and representation. All men over the age of 30, except paupers and servants without their own household, were given the right to vote: that is, about 73 per cent of men above 30 years, a percentage that gradually increased over time. Denmark introduced one of the most liberal suffrage systems in Europe at that time.[7] However, elections were open until 1901, thus causing a potential social pressure on (peasant) voters to vote according to the wishes of their masters and employers. But as underprivileged groups of the electorate grew stronger, politically as well as organizationally, one might as well imagine that open voting disfavoured the economically superior, that the pressure in fact was turned the other way. Voting was either written or "oral", and only in the first case were votes counted. In every election, voters rallied in open meetings in each election district and voted by showing hands for their candidate: voting was written only upon demand from any of the voters. Written voting became more and more common over time, and was the only practical way of voting after secret voting was introduced in 1901.

Sweden and Finland were much slower to reach popular democracy, Finland because of its historic traditions acquired as a part of Sweden, but mostly because of the Russian czarist oppression in the period after 1809. Both countries maintained estate-representation for a remarkably long time, Sweden until 1866, and Finland until 1906 (but no elections were held prior to 1863). In Sweden each estate had its own rules, which differed from region to region, for choosing representatives in the period 1809-1865. However, it can be generally stated that the following groups were entitled to vote: all independent farmers; clergymen (c. 2500-3000); burghers who paid local tax; and noblemen (c. 900 families in 1865). The votes of the burghers were graded in proportion to the amount of tax paid. After the Parliament Act of 1866, members of the First Chamber were elected or appointed by *landstingen* and *stadsfullmäktige,* who were themselves elected through communal elections in which men and women could vote, votes being graded in proportion to tax paid, and in which private firms could also vote. Suffrage for the Second Chamber was based upon tax, income and property: those who had communal voting rights *and* who owned property of a specified value *or* a farm of a certain value *or* who paid tax to the state of a given minimum income. Only men were entitled to vote. Sweden adopted the lowest age requirement of the four countries: no voting age was specified in the Parliament Act, but 21 years of age was adopted in practice. The voting age was *raised* in 1908. About 22 per cent of men of age qualified for voting in 1872, a proportion that increased to 35 per cent in 1908, when rules were liberalized. It is quite remarkable that Sweden democratized so slowly, since Norway had possessed far more liberal rules for 50 years, and Denmark even more liberal rules for 17 years when Sweden discussed and effected a parliamentary reorganization in 1866. Finland made an unusual jump from estate-representation, with about 18 per cent of adult males enfranchised in 1904, to a one-chamber parliament with universal adult suffrage in 1906. Finland was at once the most democratized of the four countries.

Thresholds of incorporation are assumed to have effects upon the timing and level of political mobilization. The earlier the democratization, the earlier the growth of mass parties, and a mobilization of voters may be expected. The lower the threshold of incorporation, and the more differentiated the society as a whole, the more differentiated the interests that are supposed to be represented in parliament, and the greater the need for organization and mobilization. Finally, the more interests that are represented, the scarcer the resources per interest, thus creating the need for a mobilization to support any interest. However, early democratization by itself, independent of the development of parties, should make for the earlier mobilization of voters who become accustomed to elections and are placed under some pressure to vote. For example, one might expect participation rates to reach higher levels earlier in Norway than in Sweden when the electorates in the two countries have reached similar size, relatively speaking. Likewise, one might expect mass parties to evolve earlier in Denmark and Norway than in Sweden.

TABLE 1. COMPARATIVE TABLE OF VOTING REQUIREMENTS (—AGE)*

	DENMARK (Folketing only, 1849–)	FINLAND (The Diet of estates 1809–1904, Eduskunta 1907–)	NORWAY (Storting 1814–)	SWEDEN (Estate assembly 1809–1865, Riksdagen 2nd Chamber 1866–)
Positively defined criteria of inclusion:				
Sex	men 1849– women 1918–	men 1809– women 1907–	men 1814– women 1915–	men 1809– women 1921–
Tax			1885–97 citizens paying taxes on income above given minima	1809–65: Burghers paying local tax; votes graded
Income				1866–1908: persons having a taxable income above given minima
Property		1809–1904: Burghers and peasants; votes graded in prop. to tax paid	1814–97: freehold and leasehold farmers, owners of urban property	1809–65: indep. farmers. 1866–1908: farmers owning property of specified value
Estate Criteria, Social Position	All men not being servants or farm helpers	1809–1904: Nobility, heads of families; Clergy, bishops and priests, 1872–1904: civil servants	1814–97: King's officials and citizens licensed as artisans	1809–65: Nobility, heads of families, clergymen
Formal education		1872–1904: University teachers, school teachers		
Negatively defined criteria of exclusion: Bankruptcy, economic reasons			1814–1914: bankruptcy	1866–1921: those who owed taxes. 1909–45: bankruptcy
Receivers of poor relief, Public ass.	1849–1915		1900–19	1909–21 (modified), –45 (ended)
Manhood suffrage	In practice: 1901	1907–	In practice: 1900–	In practice: 1911–
Universal suffrage	1918–	1907–	1915–	1921–

*Major source: Rokkan and Meyriat (1969)

"**The political system**". A clarifying note on the terminology employed is necessary. The indicators of social mobilization and indicator of political participation will not always refer to the same "population" or "system". If we regard the whole population of a nation to constitute the "social system", and those who have the right to vote to be members of the "political system", we have two analytically distinct systems of which the political always will be the smaller one. One may describe the political development in a society to be "democratic" whenever the political system grows proportionally more than the social system, though this should not be interpreted literally: variations in birth and death rates may cause "disturbances". A measure of "democraticness" would be the proportion of the members of the social system who are also members of the political system. Nations, in which this proportion is about 60-65 (dependent upon demographic structure), can be referred to as "mass democracies" (only persons below the age of 18 to 21 would be disqualified to vote).

All the Nordic countries have developed into mass democracies, and have in fact lived up to this characteristic for more than 50 years. But the boundaries of the political system have been widened at different time-points, at different pace and in different scope. When studying the historical development of political participation, it can be useful to divide the modern political histories of the countries into political time periods, to be defined by such macro-constraints as suffrage rules. Since the chosen indicator of political participation always relates voting turnout to the size of the electorate ("the political system") at any time, it is obvious that the degree of participation will be influenced by the scope of suffrage extensions and by the level of social mobilization at the time of the widening of the political system. The division into political time periods will make possible a cross-national comparison of approximately analogous political time periods.

Indicators of social mobilization will have the "social system" as basis of reference. This is not wholly satisfactory since the dependent variable operates within the framework of the "political system". However, it may be justifiable to assume that the level of social mobilization is "equal" in both the "non-political" and the "political" parts of the social system, or at least that a change in the level of social mobilization affects the two systems to the same degree. And if this assumption is dubious, then our second assumption would be that the indicators of social mobilization are more valid for measuring changes in the "political" system than in the "non-political".

The notion of "political time". in everyday conversations we happen to use concepts like "inter-war period", "war period" and "post-war period".

And likewise: "the Renaissance", "the Victorian era", "the Middle Ages". The habit of dividing *time* into distinguishable periods is prevalent within all scientific fields, and outside as well. This is because what we call "chronological", "calendar" or "astronomical" time has relatively little meaning in itself.[8] This work, for instance, is a study of what we might term "the modern history" of the Nordic countries, and by employing this concept, nobody should expect any description of developments 500 years back in time, although this span of time is trifling in the history of mankind. Conceptualization of time helps to render common frames of understanding.

We want to identify some common criterion by which we are able to divide chronological time into periods both for the purpose of studying different periods of time cross-temporally and for comparing analogous periods cross-sectionally. Or to be concrete: the development of suffrage rules has been fairly similar in some of the Nordic countries. It is possible to periodize chronological time on the basis of level of political democratization. In this way, we can compare a "political time period 1" with a "political time period 2" within one national context (what is called a study of different periods cross-temporally), and compare a "political time period 1" with another "political time period 1" cross-nationally (what in lack of better terms is called a study of analogous periods cross-sectionally). This kind of periodization is a way of supplying background information, and providing settings, within which other phenomena can be related to each other in more meaningful terms. A certain phenomenon here the scope of "the political system" is held constant. In the nordic context, it is meaningful to distinguish between three periods of "political time" defined on the basis of level of political incorporation. They are labelled "periods of democratization". For the analysis in this study, the following taxonomy is considered to have relevance:

The period 1849-1915 in Denmark is actually located somewhere between period 1 and 2, but is here tentatively divided in 1849-1901, and 1901-1915. For Denmark, Finland and Sweden, period 1 can be extended further back in time (Denmark 1834, Finland 1809, Sweden 1809), but another criterion in addition to the incorporation one, namely the "democratic" state of representative organs, has been taken into consideration. The start-years in the scheme signify the beginning of the modern constitutional histories in the four countries. The first period in Finland has been placed in parentheses, partly because participation data are lacking, and partly because of the status of dependence upon Russia in that particular period.

Figure 2 Operationalization of political time periods

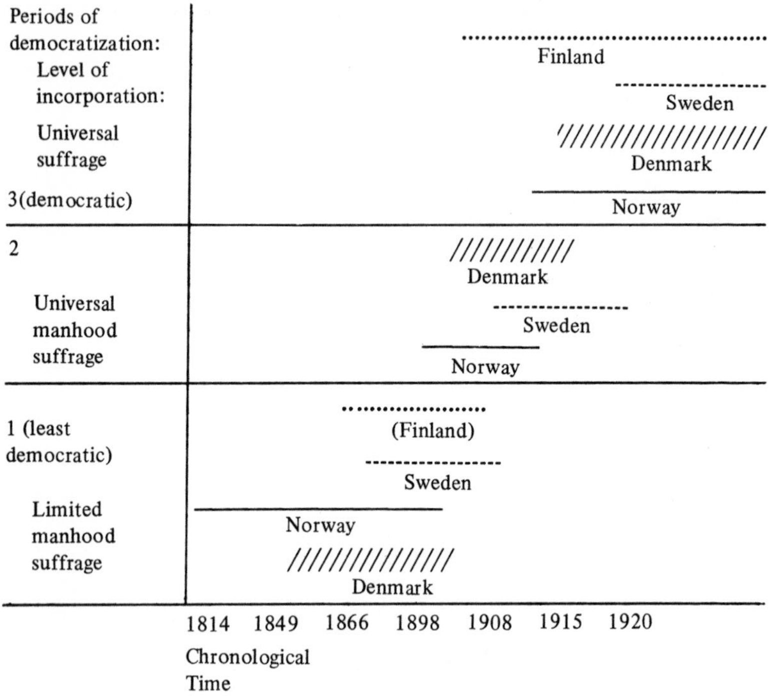

Political time periods as settings for a comparison of participation patterns. The political time periods defined have been used as settings for a comparison of participation trends cross-temporally and cross-sectionally. The hypothesis is that: political participation increases over time (that is, it is highly correlated with chronological time), and shows similar growth patterns in all systems. No series of turnout data exists for estate-elections in Finland, so Finland is listed only in time phase 3, universal suffrage.

Table 2 shows some striking similarities between corresponding time periods in the four countries. Participation patterns in the three countries in period 1 look remarkably similar with respect to lowest, average and highest turnout. Though the Swedish period is timed later chronologically, its turnout rates seem to lag behind turnout rates in Norway. This pattern is wholly in line with the argument on relationships between level of social mobilization and political participation: Norway experienced an earlier social mobilization. The growth rate, as measured by B in the regression equation, is higher for Sweden, but is accounted for by the fewer number of elections in the period. Denmark has the highest average turnout,

TABLE 2. POLITICAL PARTICIPATION IN THE NORDIC COUNTRIES: POLITICAL TIME PERIODS AS SETTINGS

Political time period	Country	Chronological time	Lowest turnout	Average	Highest turnout	The B in linear regression equation*	Turnout correlated with chronolog. time	No of cases (= elections)
1	Denmark	1849–98	15.6	43.2	72.2	0.95	0.89	24
	Norway**	1814–97	26.6	36.8	72.2	0.42	0.67	24
	Sweden***	1866–1908	19.1	37.0	61.3	1.09	0.92	14
2	Denmark	1901–13	56.5	67.4	74.8	1.71	0.94	6
	Norway	1900–13	54.6	57.2	60.4	0.40	0.63	5
	Sweden	1911–20	55.3	62.8	69.9	− 0.40	− 0.21	5
3	Denmark****	1915–	74.7	81.7	89.0	0.21	0.81	21
	Finland	1907–	50.7	66.3	84.9	0.39	0.75	24
	Norway	1915–	55.8	74.3	85.0	0.42	0.82	15
	Sweden	1921–	53.0	75.0	88.7	0.64	0.93	15

*   Average increase in percentage-points per year (*not* election year)
**   Data not available before 1829
***   Data not available before 1872
**** Data missing for 1915

another confirmation of the postulated effects of earlier social mobilization.

Time period 2 is brief in all three cases, counting in each case only 5 and 6 elections. But again one is struck by the similar turnout patterns, with Denmark in the "lead". Sweden has now passed Norway; this was not to be expected from a comparison of data on level of social mobilization, but the *tempo* of social mobilization was fast in Sweden in this period. Special notice should be made of the negative slope in the Swedish case. This fact is contrary to expectation, and hard to explain on the basis of social mobilization data. It is also contrary to the common belief that turnout rates decrease in the first election(s) after an extension of the suffrage: turnout decreased very little from 1908 to 1911, increasing sharply in the spring election of 1914, before decreasing gradually until universal suffrage was introduced for the 1921 election.

Time period 3 illustrates very clearly the relationships between social mobilization (data: see section IV) and political participation, as well as the similar participation trends in the four countries. All countries have reached approximately the same turnout levels in the late 1960s, and the data on social mobilization indicate not only that all countries have reached high levels *per se* in a global perspective (cf. the distributions from Russett et al. (1964)) but also that the inter-nation differences have narrowed. Both socio-economically, and politically (considering also party-systems), the countries now present very similar structures.

Development of Mass Parties

A distinction is frequently drawn between élite parties and mass parties. By élite party is understood a kind of organization that exists at the élite level only. A mass party is an organization that makes great efforts to build up a nationwide set of local branches to mobilize, among other things, voters for support in general elections. An élite party works within the parliament only: élite groupings, or a gathering of common interests in some loose organization, are supposed to grow in any representative organ (though the concept "party" is usually saved for more formal organizations). LaPalombara and Weiner (1966: 6) offer a suitable definition of party. They state that for an organization to be defined as a party requires (1) *continuity* in organization; (2) *manifest* and presumably *permanent* organization at the local level; (3) self-conscious determination of leaders at both national and local levels to *capture* and to *hold decision-making power*; (4) a concern on the part of the organization for *seeking followers* at the polls. The second and fourth criterion are seen as the most important for our purpose, which is to describe the emergence of *mass* parties. In the brief discussion in the last section, it was stated that other things being equal mass parties would be more likely to emerge earlier in systems with wide suffrage rules than in systems with a restricted enfranchisement. In the period 1850-1900, Denmark had the most liberal enfranchisement of the four countries, and was also the first to experience social mobilization. Mass parties also appeared in Denmark earlier than in the other three countries. As early as the 1870s, farmers united, though with constant internal dissension, in *Det Forenede Venstre.* A conservative, town-based counterpart developed in the middle of the decade. A social democratic movement had great difficulty in establishing itself during the 1870s, but nevertheless was formally organized in 1878, and gained representation in *Folketinget* from 1884 onwards, 12 years earlier than in Sweden, and 20 years earlier than in Norway. An urban wing of the *Venstre* party seceded in 1905, and the old liberal party was transformed to an agrarian party.

The first party organizations in Norway were established in 1882-84: a liberal *Venstre,* based on farmers and urban intellectuals, and a conservative *Høire,* primarily based on the emerging industrial and commercial classes in the towns and higher civil servants. The liberal party has constantly experienced splits ever since its foundation: 1888 ("Moderates"); 1892 ("The Centre"); 1903 ("Liberals"); 1909 ("National Liberals"); all of which gradually joined the Conservatives. Later, one split occurred along the functional conflict dimension and one along the cultural dimension: the Farmers' Party broke away in 1920 and the Christian People's Party 1933. In 1972, yet another split of the old liberal party took place, this time more or less as a result of the debate over Norway joining the European Common Market. The Social Democratic Party was formed closely after the two "bourgeois" parties in 1887.

Sweden was dominated by élite *(Riksdags)* parties in the first period after the disappearance of estate representation. *Lantmannapartiet,* based on farmers' support, dominated the Second Chamber in the early years after the representation reform. In 1887 there was a serious split between Protectionists and Free Traders within the party. This event triggered off what possibly could be called the first mass party mobilization, and the "Old" (Free Traders) and the "New" (Protectionists) *Lantmannapartiet* existed until 1895, when the two parties re-united, in principle as a conservative party. A social democratic party organization appeared in 1889, but functioned mainly as an élite grouping during its first years. The liberal and conservative parties existing today organized in the first decade after the turn of the century. A Farmers' Party emerged in 1915. It is worth noticing that in the official statistics the distribution of votes by party are listed only from 1911.

When the Finnish *Lantdag* assembled again in 1863, a wave of national sentiments swept across the country, aroused by the cultural ideologist Snellmann in Åbo (Turku). Language and education were politicized, and several political groups organized themselves in the latter part of the 19th century. Party mobilization was of some significance within the estates of the farmers and the burghers, but "modern" mass parties emanated only as a result of the strained relationships with Russia at the turn of the century. A labour party was formed in 1899, and reorganized as the Finnish Social Democratic Party in 1903. The fight against the czarist régime sparked the growth of mass parties. Swedish Liberals and the "Young Finns" united on a constitutionalist line, resisting Russian subversive policies, while the "Old Finns" tried to win national independence by making concessions to the Russians. Though the Social Democrats were heavily influenced by international class-war ideologies (Kautsky), they stressed the importance of national sovereignty, and associated principally with the "constitutionalists". A radical wing of the party rejected this "revisionist" policy, and was in practice more in line with the "Old Finns". Yet another party, the peasants' party was established on a socio-economic basis. The period of russification from 1894 onwards created a strong political consciousness among the general public. And when universal suffrage was introduced in 1906, resulting in one million new voters, a fairly high participation rate could be expected. As a result of its struggle for constitutional rights and greater socio-economic justice, Finland both attained the most democratic suffrage system of the Nordic countries, and produced a fully-fledged, modern party system. Communist parties emerged in all countries in 1920-1921, and all countries experienced the rise and fall of fascist parties in the 1930s.

The structures of the party systems of today are generally the same everywhere: a social democratic, a conservative, an agrarian, and a liberal (in Norway recently two) party. A communist party exists in all countries, but is particularly strong only in Finland, while socialist parties also exist in all countries. Two distinctive parties are the Swedish People's party in Finland and the Christian People's party in Norway.

In the next Section, the formation of mass parties will be depicted as a result of a process of social mobilization. No strict model is postulated, and no strict statistical testing of the postulated relationships is possible. However, a study of social mobilization data and electoral turnout data should yield clues to the general probability of the stated proposition. Since Denmark was the first of the four countries to have mass parties, one might interpret this as a sign of early social mobilization. Norway too should be expected to have slightly earlier social mobilization than Sweden.

Level of political participation as an effect of the establishment of mass parties. The hypothesis to be tested is: Establishment of modern mass parties will have a catalytic effect on political participation. "Catalytic" implies an expectation of a significant increase in the level of political participation. By "significant" we shall mean an increase in proportion participating of at least 15 per cent from the immediate election *before* establishment of parties to the immediate election *after*. The hypothesis will be tested on nation-level for three nations: Finland has to be excluded due to lack of data for pre-party period. The dates marking the emergence of mass parties in the three other countries are set at 1870 in Denmark, 1882 in Norway, and 1887 in Sweden. A simple method was chosen to illustrate the immediate effect of the establishment of mass parties: linear regression lines were drawn for the pre-party period and the post-party establishment period. The number of elections included in the post-party period was equal to the number defined by data-availability for the pre-party period.[9]

The estimations showed that the establishment of mass parties had an *immediate* effect on mobilization: from the last election *before* parties were launched to the first election *after,* turnout increased by about 10 percentage-points in Denmark, 18 in Norway, and 25 in Sweden. This is not to be interpreted solely as an effect of the existence and activity of party organizations as such. The mere emergence and formation of parties is a sign of interest conflicts becoming more visible and more profound. A party organization is a tool or an agency to aggregate common interests. The need to mobilize potential voters gains importance. Mobilization comes about as a result of mobilizing agencies establishing themselves and political issues being discussed and regarded as crucial.

The average per cent turnout increased considerably between the two periods in all three countries:

	Denmark	Norway	Sweden
pre-party period	29.8 (12 elections)	30.2 (18 elections)	21.6 (5 elections)
post-party period	56.6 (12 elections)	60.9 (18 elections)	42.0 (5 elections)

The importance of including formal party data in explaining political mobilization is demonstrated. The figures above illustrate that political mobilization was slower and more gradual in Sweden than in the two other countries. This may not be a confirmation of the hypothesis, but is certainly consistent with the thoughts about differential effects on political mobilization of different histories of national independence and continuity of representative organs. Comparing the Norwegian pre-party period with the Swedish, turnout in Norway is higher in all elections, even though the chronological time period in Norway is 1829-1879 vs. 1872-1884 in Sweden. The turnout curve of the Danish pre-party period is the most irregular of all, turnout varying between 15 and 42 per cent, but the frequency of elections — 12 elections during a time span of 20 years — must also be considered. It was also a period with strained relations with Prussia — including two wars.

III. THEORETICAL CONCEPTIONS AND INTERPRETATION OF INDICATORS

A Search for General Sources of Political Mobilization

Institutional heritage was considered to have effect on the initial political mobilization after the major steps towards democratic representative rule were taken. These "major steps" have been associated with the year 1814 in Norway; 1849 in Denmark; 1866 in Sweden; and 1907 in Finland.

But the effect of institutional heritage and histories of state building is not considered a lasting one. Historical-political context is relevant for an understanding of *start*-levels of political mobilization. We shall argue that the *development* of rates of political participation is dependent upon social mobilization. Two aspects of social mobilization will be related to political participation: level and tempo. A theoretical perspective on political participation is sketched. While we so far have outlined early mobilization as an effect of *specific* national historical developments, we shall now try to identify *general* sources of mobilization patterns by considering the entire period until 1970.

Political Participation as a Diffusion Process

The process of increasing political participation will be termed political mobilization. This terminology implies that "somebody" and/or "something" is understood to mobilize, or have a mobilizing effect on, somebody else (those who previously have not taken part in political life). The "somebody" or "something" are conditions for the still-not-participants to take an interest in political institutions (e.g., elections to National Assembly) and move into the groups of active participants. The "somebody" may be élite groups or party organizations. They can sometimes be regarded as mobilizers or mobilizing agencies. One of the main tasks of emerging political parties is to mobilize non-voters and to persuade old and new voters to vote for certain policy alternatives. Some attention has already been paid to the timing of the establishment and appearance of mass parties on the electoral scene. What mobilizing effects do parties and party competition have? The establishment of mass parties must in itself be interpreted as a politicization and mobilization process taking place within the political system, reflecting interest conflicts between different groups. With the emergence of political parties, we found marked increases in the proportions of the electorates voting.

The "something" may be what we have called social mobilization. Structural differentiation, social and geographical mobility, improvements in standard of living, growth of new media of mass communications – all work together to change the objective and subjective positions of people. These processes of change advance the development of new demands, and may create both new awareness (for example of relative deprivation) and new pressures (e.g., penetration, interaction) towards institutions regulating, controlling and influencing decisions on such demands. Assuming that economic resources are scarce in the build-up phase of nations, different groups will contend to seize power-holding positions thereby stimulating active participation in politics. The relationship between mobilization, mass parties and political participation, can, in a very generalized form, be schematized as follows:[10]

Figure 3. A conceptual model of political mobilization

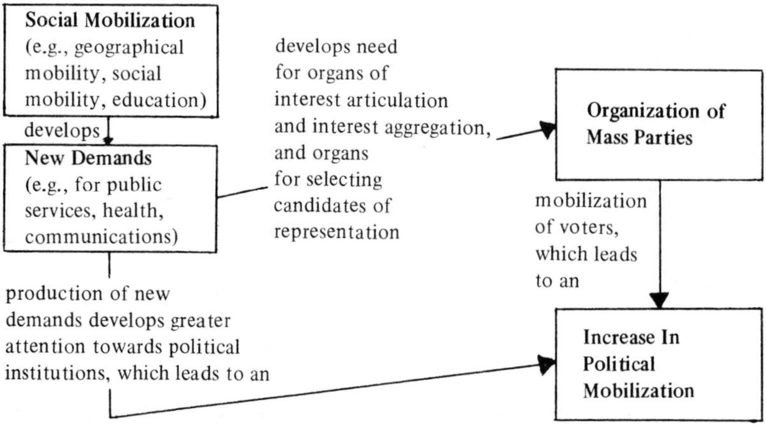

Political mobilization will be described as a process of diffusion. This is a rather unusual approach to the study of this phenomenon, and demands some explanation. The processes of social mobilization and the mobilizing effects of political parties have been postulated to mediate a greater degree of attention towards political participation. Our hypothesis will be that individuals, once sufficiently mobilized to participate in an election, will continue in the voting habit thereafter. The conception will be that once you have crossed the passive-active threshold, you do not step back to the ranks of the passive citizens. The act of voting develops into a habit. Once an individual is inculcated into the habit, he "accepts" it and internalizes it. This is a theoretical statement. The degree to which it holds true empirically is difficult to test, but an effort will be made to adapt the empirical curve of mobilization to a theoretical one.

We can think of political participation, here operationalized as the habit of voting, as a phenomenon that spreads: a. over time; b. over a territory; c. over a social structure. Points b. and c. can actually be considered sub-points of the first. Over time, political participation will increase at a different pace in different parts of a territory — the usual conception being that the habit of voting is something that is developed in the "centre", and gradually spreads to and is taken up by people in the "periphery". Over time, the habit of voting will spread from higher social classes to lower, partly because early suffrage rules kept lower classes out of the political system, thereby giving the higher classes a time-lead to internalize the habit, and partly because social mobilization affects the upper classes first. "Time" is not an independent variable in itself, but rather a setting, within which social mobilization will be considered as the phenomenon that "pushes" the level of political participation upwards. In this study, emphasis will be put on the two first points: (1) to study political participation as a process of diffusion over time, using the national territory as a unit; (2) and to study the penetration of the habit of voting throughout the national territories. The general conception of the process of diffusion of political participation has been drawn in Figure 4.[11] We can postulate that this conception is valid for territories having a history of gradual widening of the political system; that is, more and more people have gradually been incorporated and given the right to vote. A exemplifies the curve of participation in the "centre", B is the curve in a more peripheral region. Centre and periphery may be defined geographically where the distance from the geographical region of the political centre is decisive, or the concepts may be defined in terms of levels of social mobilization in different regions, or in terms of social groups (socio-economic status).[12] The two first definitions will be applied. Our conception of electoral turnout as a diffusion process should be understood within the historical context chosen. We may now have reached a "peak" state of nationhood, other organizations and other forms of participation growing more important. We could imagine processes of de-institutionalization (or *re*-institutionalization) and consequent processes of de-contagion in electoral participation.

Figure 4. A theoretical view of the general form of the curve of participation as a diffusion process

A = for example the curve of a central region

B = for example the curve of a peripheral region

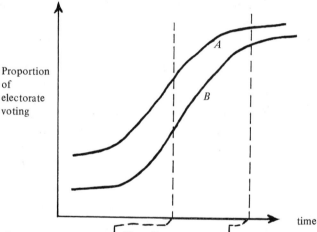

Phase I:
"LATENCY"-phase. Low level of and slow tempo of social mobilization, pre-mass-party period, restrictions on suffrage, not a great need for privileged groups to use a right denied unprivileged masses that are disqualified to offer any competition.

Phase II:
In Rostowian terms: the "TAKE-OFF" of political participation. Accelerating social mobilization, suffrage extensions, establishment and build-up of mass-party organizations which have a catalytic effect on participation.

Phase III:
"MASS PARTICIPATION". High level of social mobilization, universal suffrage, a consolidated party-system, the habit of voting ("voice") being widely accepted, parties have developed "loyalties". (The concept of "voice" and "loyalty" are borrowed from Hirschman (1970)).

Levels of political participation. In the analysis of social mobilization and political participation, we shall centre on two aspects of interrelationships: (1) level of social mobilization vs. level of political participation; (2) tempo or intensity of social mobilization vs. spurts in political participation.

This focus demands a definition of "level" of political participation. We have decided to distinguish between three levels: low, medium, high – corresponding to the three phases of participation sketched in Figure 4. The level is *low* if less than 45 per cent of qualified voters cast their votes in national elections (to the Lower House, if any); the level is *medium* if turnout is between 45 and 70 per cent; and *high* if above 70 per cent. This is not a completely arbitrary or intuitive operationalization. It is obvious that this classification would be of little interest, unless we know that there exists a reasonable empirical probability for cases to fall into one of these categories. To check the "empirical probability" we have consulted Russett et al. (1964: 84-85), who present a ranking of 100 nations on the variable "votes as percentage of voting-age population" (the election year in most cases being within the range 1957-1962). On the basis of that table, the distribution of nations on the three categories turned out to be: *low*: 37 (of which 8 are listed 0 per cent); *medium*: 19; and *high*: 44.

Spurts of political participation. In Figure 4, political participation was conceived as a diffusion process in time and space. This conception does not imply an expectation of a completely smooth curve. The possible effect of parties and of social mobilization has been touched. In addition several other events, political or economic, within the national territory or in the international environment, and all factors relating to the individual qualified voters before and on election day combine to produce an irregular curve of participation. We are interested in searching out the "positive" irregularities: these are called *spurts* in political participation.

This is not the place for an extensive introduction to diffusion processes and studies in general, or to outline the differences between the great number of equations and models of curvefitting (for a recent, thorough discussion: see Østbye, 1972). Rather, we shall discuss the model that is considered to be the most relevant to our theoretical conception. There are an extremely large number of trend types available, and the decision on which to use is not easy. But as suggested in Figure 4, we expect the level of participation to flatten out. That information makes it reasonable to search for an asymptotic growth curve. The theoretical notion of what processes are in force is an oversimplification, and we shall use a frequently mentioned analogy to serve the purpose of illustration – namely the diffusion of an infectious disease in a society. The "habit", or "practice", of voting can be viewed as being "contagious". A disease will develop in one place, among a limited number of persons. These people will infect other people, who again will infect still others, until theoretically all people have been infected. The conditions for the "success" of this process of "contagion" will depend upon the subjective and objective "physical state" of the non-infected people at any time-point. Or to speak in more familiar terms, the spread of the habit of voting is dependent upon: (1) the fact that somebody has discovered the utility of such a habit, taken it up, and started to communicate the goods and evils of this habit to others;[13] (2) and the chances of the still-not-participants being affected by the habit. People who have become socially mobile have a higher probability of being affected; we should therefore expect the habit to be more frequent in areas having a high level of social mobilization than in areas with a low level, and for it to spread more quickly in areas undergoing rapid social mobilization than in areas *not* experiencing such a process of change, or only a *slow* process. The analogy above is not valid in one respect: the "population" in our case is a shifting (and increasing) electorate − several generations are included. In classic diffusion models, the population is constant and the diffusion process is regarded to take place within a limited time-span.

The assumption is that the probability of *being* a voter increases over time, while the probability of *becoming* one decreases (there are fewer and fewer non-voters left to "infect"). Our notion is further than once having been affected by the habit, there is no way back: you will become addicted to voting! This is one of the theoretical assumptions that has to be made. If the probability of moving from the "non-affected" state (not-yet-participants) to the "affected" state (participants) had been equal at any point in time in the diffusion process, that would have been a prerequisite for describing the process as a diffusion in an homogeneous population. But as discussed under (2) above, this probability is not considered to be equal.

What we opt for then is a curve that can describe a process of "Non-Homogeneous Diffusion" (Hernes, 1972: 173-182). Hernes also suggested that his model, or a modified version, might be applied to political mobilization. He himself applied it to describe the process of entry into first marriage, while Østbye (1972) applied it to describe the diffusion of televisions in Norway. The equation for this model is:

$$P_t = \cfrac{1}{1 + \cfrac{(1 - P_0) \exp (A/\log b)}{P_0 \exp (Ab^t / \log b)}} \qquad (1)^{14}$$

which can be reduced to:

$$P_t = \cfrac{1}{1 + \cfrac{(1 - P_0) a}{P_0 a^{b^t}}} \qquad (2)^{14}$$

where P_t = in our case: the proportion of the electorate affected by the habit of voting (operationalized e.g., percentage turnout or the raw number of voters) at time t; a is derived from the formula $\log a = \dfrac{A}{\log b}$ where A is the average initial potentiality of being "affected"; b = the constant proportion of decline in this potentiality for each time unit. The above formula can be still further reduced, introducing the parameter k, the upper asymptotic value, defined as $k = P_0/(a\,[1 - P_0])$:

$$P_t = \cfrac{1}{1 + \cfrac{1}{ka^{b^t}}} \qquad (3)^{14}$$

As the first year of the process, we have to take t_0 (which will be a different year for each nation), and to assume P_0 to be higher than zero but less than 1, which indicates that the process has already started at the time-point our description starts. Furthermore, time must be considered a discrete variable, with election-years used as units. Since this diffusion process stretches over several different "political time periods" (as defined in Section II; the potential number of voters increases in an uneven tempo), we shall apply three measures of P:

(1) $P =$ $\dfrac{\text{no. of voters} \times 100}{\text{no. of qualified}}$ (percentages – ignoring the changes in electorate)

(2a) $P =$ no. of voters (raw figures – disregarding the number of non-voters, and the proportions. NB: Raw figure in the latest election has had to be set equal to 100, and all other raw figures are proportions of this)

(2b) $P =$ no. of qualified voters (see note for 2a)

2a and 2b are to be used in combination. Whenever the deviance between the empirical value and the theoretical, calculated one is *positive in both instances,* we will define this to be a case of spurt in political participation. When the deviance is positive in instance 2a, but negative in instance 2b, one can speak of a *minor* spurt. The definition of the other two outcomes: a "-", "+", or a "-", "-" follows from the above definitions. The three measures of P are suggested to enable a comparison of the results: does the choice of P have any consequences for the identification of spurts?

This is the approach chosen to identify spurts in political participation. If it turns out that the fit between the empirical and theoretical curves is bad, this could mean that the choice of model is wrong, or that political participation *cannot* be described as a process of diffusion. Whatever conclusion we may come to as to the diffusion aspect, the described method will possibly be appropriate to identify spurts.[15]

Indicators of Social Mobilization

Among the processes that can be considered to be parts of the more comprehensive phenomenon of social mobilization, we have decided to concentrate on three. These are: urbanization, economic development, and spread of education.

Urbanization

According to Lampard (1965), we can distinguish between three basic definitions of urbanization: (a) *a behavioural definition.* The concept is related to individuals, certain ways of behaving and thinking can be described as being "urban", independent of the individuals' location. (b) *a structural definition,* where the process of urbanization is characterized through changes in the occupational structure and the balance between the labour force sectors. (c) *a demographic definition,* where urbanization is considered to be a process of concentration of population.

The behavioural definition is relevant, but offers problems of data and measurement. The implications of our idea of urbanization are: that people become mobile and have to adjust to new patterns of life, and secondly that a concentration of population leads to other forms of communication between people, and that people are exposed to more and a greater variety of sources and influences, all of which may lead to behavioural patterns different from those prominent in the countryside. The last definition above covers our purposes: to measure the consequences of the fact that more and more people leave their traditional (in terms of economic and cultural life) surroundings in sparsely-populated areas and move to urban areas and towns. The process described by the structural definition will in our scheme be placed under the heading "economic development". Though a transfer of labour force from the primary to other economic sectors involves a concentration of population, it does not always have the same implications for behavioural patterns as the growth of towns. The definition is straightforward and simple, but is not without problems when operationalized. The problem arises when the boundaries between town and country disappear. How to mark the town off from the country? What about suburban areas which at least functionally are parts of towns? Due to lack of detailed data on development of population centres in the four countries,[16] a political-administrative operationalization of a town will be employed. The development of suburban areas, boundary changes, or the size of the town areas at different time-points will not be touched upon here. Urbanization, or degree of urbanization, will here mean: per cent of total population living in towns, as these at any time are defined by administrative authorities.[17]

Economic development

We are interested in variables which indicate a process of economic modernization: a development towards a money economy, change in the society's economic basis and economic organization, increases in the income and production value of the nation, improvements in people's standard of living, separation of people's home and their work-place (people do not work isolated on the farm they live, but work together with other people in factories and firms in the secondary and tertiary sector). The processes are not necessarily uni-dimensional; it is quite obvious that the proportion of gross investments of GDP may increase without implying a percentage decrease of labour force employed in the primary sector.

The process termed "economic development" is very close to "that kind of social change that leads in the direction of the liberation of a man from direct contact with nature in the production process and permits him to pursue other interests" (Galtung, 1971: 5). This process implies what is often called a transition from nature to culture. Here it will also signify a mobilization and integration process. People are being integrated into a larger system, or rather, several different "supra-local" systems. This process is assumed to lead to greater awareness of the political institutions; demands for more services will be put forward and political participation will increase.

As indicators of the kind of socio-economic development touched on, we have decided on these: (a) per cent of total labour force employed in the secondary and tertiary sector. Secondary and tertiary occupations are usually defined as all occupations not involving extraction of raw materials from nature (but "mining" is classified as "secondary"); (b) gross investments as a percentage of GDP (Gross Domestic Product); (c) GDP per capita. Indicator (b) is a common measure for the productivity aspect of economic development. GDP per capita is used to express the average amount of economic value at the disposal of the individual members of the society, or the social system under study. It will be used as a measure of standard of living, and general welfare, although one should be aware of the fact that it does not measure the *distribution* of economic resources in the society.

Spread of education

The change from being illiterate to the level of being able to read and write implies a very important qualitative change in people's subjective and objective position in society. Education increases what might be called people's "action potential" in a society: people can assert themselves in more fields than as illiterates, and people can be more easily reached by the messages of others. Education increases people's ability to mobilize resources (people, money, knowledge) and increases people's chances of being mobilized by others. The fact that people seek education beyond the elementary level helps to increase people's knowledge about and awareness of the greater society and systems outside the immediate, local world. It will be assumed that such a "wakening" will make people more mobile and increase their propensity to break up from traditional settings, especially as a socio-economic development as suggested above will make technical skills and theoretical knowledge more important resources in society.

The most common measure on the spread of education is per cent of population (15 years +) able to read and write (literates). All of the Nordic countries developed very early in this respect (see Mulhall, 1884: 157; Cipolla, 1969: 14, 96-97), and possibly as a consequence of that, no good statistics on illiteracy are available for Denmark, Norway and Sweden. The census statistics in Finland contain some figures for selected years, and indicate that Finland was a latecomer in a Nordic perspective but not compared with the majority of the European nations.

The following variables will be used as indicators of the general level of education in society at different time-points: (a) pupils in secondary schools in per cent of population aged 15-19. Age-group 15-19 may not be the most adequate measure of standardization, as 13-14 year-olds and 20 year-olds may also be enrolled as pupils sometimes. Possibly an age group 14-19, or 14-18 would be better measures of standardization, but statistical sources do not offer such splits. (b) students enrolled in higher education (post-secondary) as a pro mille of population aged 20-24. The duration of post-secondary education varies from field to field, over time-periods, and individually, but the measure of standardization is probably the most adequate. None of these indicators measures the functions of the educational systems or the content of the education. When did important institutional changes occur? When were central school-laws passed? In this round we have confined ourselves to giving the quantitative figures. The spread of education is also meant to cover the "cultural" component of the phenomenon of social mobilization.

Levels of social mobilization. The next step is to evaluate and interpret different *values* for the indicators. The objective is to set up a tabular scheme of analysis, whereby three levels of social mobilization can be differentiated for each of the indicators. The three levels will be labelled low, medium and high (abbreviated: L, M, H). The definition of levels has been based on qualitative judgements, and checked against the "empirical probability" to be read out of the rank distributions in Russett et al. (1964) For some of the indicators it is problematic to talk about high or low levels in absolute terms. What is high today, may have been unthinkable 50 years ago, and it may be low two generations ahead. In some instances the level in the top-ranking nations in the 1960s must be considered a valid definition of "high". The conceptualization then, is constrained by observable phenomena in the present historical time period. To develop criteria that would be valid for all times is neither possible nor very useful.[18]

Four of the indicators below are allowed to vary between 0 and 100 per cent. The percentages have different meanings dependent upon which phenomenon we want to describe. In this historical time period, we are prone to characterize a nation as highly urbanized, if at least 30 per cent of its population live in towns, but also to describe the level of education in a nation to be high, when 5 per cent of all persons in age-group 20-24 attend universities or high schools. The fifth indicator, GDP per capita, can in theory grow indefinitely. This indicator creates problems because of the difficulty of cross-national and cross-temporal comparison of price-assessments. It would demand great efforts to work out comparative tables of GDP per capita with a common basis (e.g., US-$, 1960), for longer time periods. The solution chosen is extraordinary, but seems to be the best under the circumstances. For Denmark, Norway and Sweden we have data for GDP per capita in fixed prices (different years as basis in the three countries). The level in 1950 can be described as high (see below) and be set equal to 100. For earlier years, GDP per capita is calculated as a percentage of the 1950-level, and three levels of GDP per capita have been defined.

Five of the six indicators shall be employed to characterize levels of social mobilization, while all six will be used to describe tempo of social mobilization. When deciding the overall level of social mobilization at any time-point, all five indicators will be assigned equal weight. Decisions on the differentiation of levels have followed these lines:

LEVELS

Dimension	Indicator	Low	Medium	High
Urbanization	% of total population living in towns	below 20%	between 20 and 30%	above 30%
		In Russett (1964:51) a ranking of 120 nations on proportions of population in cities over 20,000 inhabitants yields this distribution:		
		65	18	37
Economic development	% of labour force employed in the secondary and tertiary sector	below 50%	between 50 and 65%	above 65%
		If we invert Russett's rank table on percentage of labour force employed in agriculture, we get this distribution of 98 nations (Russett, 1964:177):		
		57	15	26
		This is only an approximate distribution of nations by level of employment in the non-*primary* sector.		

GDP per capita	below 50% of 1950-level	between 50 and 75% of 1950-level	above 75% of 1950-level

(D.Kr., N.Kr., Sv.Kr. in fixed prices)

The argument for setting the 1950-level as high, is that in a table Russett presents of GNP per capita, 1957, $U.S., Sweden scores number 6, Norway 11 and Denmark 12 in a ranking of 122 nations (Russett, 1964:155).

Spread of education	Pupils in secondary schools in % of persons in age-group 15-19	below 10%	between 10 and 20%	above 20%

Russett's table on level of education is not directly comparable, since he has calculated primary *and* secondary school pupils as percentage of population aged 15-19. In his ranking of 125 nations, Denmark ranks 12, Sweden 14, Finland and Norway 17, in 1960 (Russett, 1964:218).

	Students at universities and high schools in ‰ of persons in age-group 20-24	below 20‰	between 20 and 40‰	above 40‰

Russett has not controlled for demographic structure. He has calculated students enrolled in higher education per 100,000 population. Of 105 nations, the Nordic countries had these ranks and values in 1960 (Russett, 1964:214):

Denmark, rank	12,570
Finland, rank	17,529
Sweden, rank	25,401
Norway, rank	44,258

The range in the table is from 1983 (U.S.A.) to 3 (Rhodesia and Nyasaland).

Tempo of social mobilization. All six indicators will be applied in the scheme of tempo of social mobilization. The format of the scheme is similar to the one invented for the analysis of levels of social mobilization. We shall distinguish between three value-categories of tempo: retarded (and/or stagnant), intermediate tempo, and accelerating, abbreviated as R, I, A. In this scheme of tempo, we are concerned about what is going on *between* two time points or two time periods (e.g., decades). Having ascertained the levels of social mobilization at time-points A, B and C, we are as much interested in the intensity of social mobilization in the time periods between A and B, and B and C. The motivation is to compare periods of acceleration with periods of spurts in political participation.

The basic measure of tempo, or intensity, will be the change in percentage points from one decade to another. In the scheme on levels, percentages were used as measures. To calculate the percentage increase-decrease of percentages, is considered not to be fruitful. Change in percentage-points is here seen to be a better way of illustrating tempo. Of course, we have to be aware of the different starting-levels on the various indicators. The higher the level of departure, the less increases in percentage-points are possible. But the hypothesis will be that the higher the start-level, the more gradual and even the social mobilization, and this again will reflect less drastic spurts in political participation.

In setting up the scheme of tempo, we shall again seek the advice of Russett et al. (1964), and also consult Deutsch (1961), who has proposed what the pattern of a country undergoing rapid social mobilization might look like. This is the proposed scheme of tempo of social mobilization:

		TEMPO		
Dimension	Indicator	Retarded	Intermediate	Accelerating
Urbanization	% of total population living in towns	Decrease, or increase in %-points less than 1.0 per decade	Increase in %-points between 1.0 and 3.5 per decade	Increase in %-points more than 3.5 per decade

Russett has a ranking on average annual change in %-points of 50 nations[19]. The time span varies a lot (from 1950–1960 to 1920–1960). A classification according to this scheme shows this picture:

| 8 | 15 | 17 |

In Deutsch's (1961) pattern a decade growth rate of 1–12 percentage-points is considered "rapid", which makes his concept of rapid a very broad one.

| *Economic development* | % of labour force employed in the secondary and tertiary sector | Decrease in %-points, or an increase of less than 3.0 per decade | Increase in %-points between 3.0 and 6.0 per decade | Increase in %-points more than 6.0 per decade |

Russett's table on average annual change in per cent of labour force employed in agriculture has been inverted, and the 49 nations adjusted to this scheme have this distribution (Russett, 1964:180):

| 12 | 17 | 20 |

In Deutsch's (1961) model, "rapid" social mobilization implies an occupational shift out of agriculture of 4–10 percentage-points per decade.

Gross investments in per cent of GDP	Average annual %-level per decade less than 12, *and* increase in %-points from former decade less than 1.0	Average annual %-level per decade between 12 and 15, *or* increase in %-points from former decade between 1.0 and 3.0	Average annual %-level per decade above 15, *or* increase in %-points more than 3.0

These operationalizations of tempo are rather complicated, but it turns out that Rostow's (1960) definitions of "take-off" – that the ratio of gross investments of national income rises from 5 to 10% is not satisfactory, or at least not sufficient as a differentiating measure of productivity.[20] In Russett's (1964:168) ranking of 77 nations on gross domestic capital formation as a percentage of GNP, only 13 had a percentage less than 12, eight between 12 and 15, and the rest, 56, above 15.[21] In addition to the ratio of GDP criterion, we have proposed the amount of change in %-points to be used in combination with the first criterion in the retardation cell, and as an alternative measure in the other two cells. An increase of 3 %-points or more, is considered an acceleration whatever the ratio is.

GDP per capita	% increase per decade less than 15	% increase per decade between 15 and 25	% increase per decade more than 25

Russett (1964:160) has a table on *annual* growth of GNP per capita, which is not wholly comparable with this scheme, but applying splits between: less than 1.5% annual increase; 1.5 to 2.5; and more than 2.5% annual increase, the following distribution of 68 nations comes out:

	15	19	34

Spread of education	Pupils in secondary schools in % of persons aged 15–19	Decrease in %-points, or an increase of less than 2.0 per decade	An increase in %-points between 2.0 and 5.0 per decade	An increase in %-points of more than 5.0 per decade

Students at universities and high schools in %₀ of persons aged 20–24	Decrease, or increase in %₀ points of less than 5.0 per decade	An increase in %₀ points of between 5.0 and 10.0 per decade	An increase in %₀ points of more than 10.0 per decade

Neither Deutsch (1961) nor Russett (1964) has any tables on changes in these educational indicators. Russett (1964:225) has one on average annual %-points increase in literacy, and the location of his 43 cases in our scheme renders this result.

13	17	13

But a change in proportion of literates is not the same thing as a change in proportion of students. Deutsch (1961) reckons an increase of 10-14%-points in literacy per decade to be "rapid" social mobilization.

HYPOTHESES

We propose to set forth the following hypotheses:

Formulation of hypothesis:

(1) Level of political participation is dependent upon level of social mobilization. High levels of political participation occur when social mobilization levels are high.

Procedure for testing:

(1) will be tested on two levels of units:

a. *nation-level* (all four nations)
The schemes of levels of political participation and social mobilization will be used. The comparison of levels will have decades as time settings.

b. *province-level* (Finland, Norway, Sweden)[22]
Data for level of urbanization and proportion of labour force employed in the secondary and tertiary sector will be correlated with data on voting turnout for as many election years as possible ("level" means here % urbanized, % in secondary + tertiary sector, % turnout – *not* low, medium, high).

(2) Spurts in political participation are dependent upon tempo of social mobilization. Spurts will occur in periods with accelerating social mobilization.

(2) will be tested according to the scheme of social mobilization and the method of identifying spurts in political participation. All four nations are included, and the time setting will be the whole "modern political period".

(3) The curves of political participation over time will have approximately similar shapes in the politically most central region and the geographical-politically most peripheral region of a nation, but there will be a difference in timing of the different phases. The "take-off" phase in the process of diffusion will be lagging in the periphery – using chronological time as setting.

(3) will be tested by the drawing of graphs of the empirical curves of political participation over a certain time span. This is not a "test" in strict terms but will offer a clear illustration of the degree to which the stated hypothesis holds true. Data for Finland, Norway and Sweden will be used, and the time-period covered depends upon the availability of data (F.: 1907–1962, N.: 1829–1969, S.: here only 1911–1960) The units of analysis will be the "central" region and the "most peripheral" one in each country.

"Centre" – "periphery" are relational concepts. Within each nation a political centre is defined, namely the capital and its immediate surroundings, and the most peripheral region will be defined as the region having the geographically most distant location from the centre.

The operationalizations of "central" and "most peripheral" regions will be:

Country:	"Central region" consists of these electoral districts	"Peripheral region" of these elect. districts
FINLAND	Helsingfors, Nylands län, Åbo-Björneborgs län (Åland included until 1919)	Lapplands län Uleåborgs län
NORWAY	Oslo, Östfold, Vestfold, Akershus	Finnmark, Troms Nordland
SWEDEN	Stockholm, Sth. län, Uppsala 1., Västman-land, Södermanland	Nordbotten, Västerbotten

IV. EMPIRICAL DATA AND TEST OF HYPOTHESES

Level of Social Mobilization vs. Level of Political Participation

Hypothesis 1: Level of political participation is dependent upon level of social mobilization. High levels of political participation occur when social mobilization levels are high.

Tested on national level. Tables 3-8 show that Denmark was the first country to begin on a social mobilization process. Already in 1800, more than 20 per cent of the population lived in towns – a proportion that

TABLE 3. LEVELS OF SOCIAL MOBILIZATION: URBANIZATION.
% OF TOTAL POPULATION LIVING IN TOWNS 1800-1960.
DENMARK, FINLAND, NORWAY AND SWEDEN.

The lines in the table mark the transitions from level L to M, and from level M to H.

Year	Denmark	Finland*	Norway**	Sweden
1800	20.9	5.0	7.4	9.8
1835	20.8	5.9	10.9	9.7
1850	20.8	6.4	12.8	10.1
1860	23.6	6.3	14.5	11.3
1870	24.8	7.5	16.9	13.0
1880	28.1	8.4	20.0	15.1
1890	33.3	9.9	23.7	18.8
1900	38.3	12.9	28.2	21.5
1910	40.3	15.5	28.9	24.8
1920	43.2	17.3	29.8	29.5
1930	44.2	20.6	28.5	32.5
1940	47.7	26.8	28.6	37.4
1950	49.5	32.3	32.3	46.6
1960	47.4	38.4	32.2	51.6

*   Data for 1835: interpolation based on data for 1830 and 1840.
** Data for 1850, 1860, 1870 and 1880 are all linear interpolations (data existing for 1845, 1855, 1865, 1875 and 1890). The figures for 1950-1960 may seem low. If all densely populated areas with 2000 inhabitants or more had been used instead or urban population, the percentage would have risen to 49 in 1960.

TABLE 4. LEVELS OF SOCIAL MOBILIZATION: ECONOMIC DEVELOPMENT I.
% OF LABOUR FORCE EMPLOYED IN THE NON-PRIMARY SECTOR
1870-1960* DENMARK, FINLAND, NORWAY AND SWEDEN.

The lines in the table mark the transitions from level L to M, and from level M to H.

Year	Denmark	Finland	Norway	Sweden
1870	48.3			26.7
1875			40.7	
1880	49.6	21.0		29.8
1890	53.1	24.0	44.7	32.8
1900	56.9	28.0	53.4	39.3
1910	60.0	30.0	53.1	49.3
1920	62.3	37.0	57.9	56.3
1930	66.9	43.0	58.9	65.3
1940	72.0	53.0		69.7
1945			66.5	
1950	77.1	58.5	71.0	79.0
1960	82.5	68.3	80.5	86.2

* Sources are generally official censuses. For Finland the data for 1880–1940 are taken from Clark (1951:416). Women in agriculture have been excluded in his labour force statistics. Data for 1950–1960 are from Nousiainen (1966:14). These figures mirror the distribution of total population among economic sectors, not the actual labour force. The figures for 1950 and 1960 are therefore possibly underestimated, since the average size of family is larger among people employed in the agricultural sector.

**TABLE 5. LEVELS OF SOCIAL MOBILIZATION: ECONOMIC DEVELOPMENT II.
GDP PER CAPITA IN % OF GDP PER CAPITA IN 1950.
DENMARK (1929 PRICES), NORWAY (1938 PRICES), SWEDEN (1913 PRICES);
1860-1950*.**

The lines mark the transitions from level L to M, and from M to H.

Year	Denmark	Norway[**]	Sweden
1860			12.7
1865		25.8	
1870	27.3		15.0
1875		32.0	
1880	32.1		17.4
1890	39.7	31.1	20.5
1900	48.9	39.1	27.0
1910	57.9	45.5	34.6
1920	64.0	55.8	42.9
1930	80.2	70.9	53.7
1940	77.1	86.8	65.9
1950	100.0	100.0	100.0

* Data for Finland missing.
** Data from 1877 has been used for 1875, from 1887 for 1890, from 1899 for 1900. Data for 1910 and 1920 are results of linear interpolations from data 1905 and 1916, and 1916 and 1926.

**TABLE 6. LEVELS OF SOCIAL MOBILIZATION: SPREAD OF EDUCATION I.
PUPILS IN SECONDARY GENERAL SCHOOLS AS A PERCENTAGE OF
PERSONS IN AGE-GROUP 15-19* 1875-1970.
DENMARK, FINLAND, NORWAY, SWEDEN.**

Year	Denmark	Finland	Norway[**]	Sweden[***]
1875		2.0	8.3	
1880	3.4 (1883)		8.5	3.1
1890	4.4 (1888)	2.9	10.3	3.3
1900	6.3 (1902)	5.4	9.5	3.4
1910	10.2	8.3	9.7	4.2
1900	12.5	9.4	12.8	5.5
1930	15.6	14.9	9.4	6.7
1940	20.3	16.3	12.6	11.3
1950	30.4	30.4	17.1	29.4
1960	29.0	53.7	39.6	
1965	25.4	52.7	35.2	34.5
1970	33.9			41.1

* These data are difficult to compare across nations. It is problematic to assess exactly how many school-classes have been included in the statistics. From 1896, pupils in Norway started their intermediate (secondary) education after the 5th year in primary school. This education lasted 4 years; after that came 3 years in *gymnasium*. From 1920, 2 (3) years of intermediate schooling followed 7 years of elementary education. The Danish and Swedish systems have been fairly similar, although I have not checked the exact years of changes. Common to all three countries have been a substantial number of mixed arrangements at any time, until the last decade. Secondary education in Finland started after 4 years in primary school: 5 years intermediate + 3 years in *gymnasium*. Since 1928, an alternative system has existed with 6 + 3/4 + 3. In Denmark, Norway and Sweden, the voluntary intermediate schooling has been gradually replaced by compulsory 8th and 9th year of primary education since about 1960. Pupils in these school classes have not been included in the statistics on secondary education. The data on Finland are therefore relatively too high in 1960–1965. Some figures from 1964 illustrate the inter-nation differences better. These figures show the proportions of 19-year-olds having finished the *gymnasium* in 1964:

Denmark:	Finland:	Norway:	Sweden:
9.2	12.9	15.8	13.2

(Source: Sandven and Sysiharju, 1966:97).

** Enrolment data for Norway: entries for school-years 1875–1876, 1880–1881, etc. indicated for the years 1875, 1880, etc. Age-group data: average number for 5-year periods 1871–75, 1876–80, etc.

*** Enrolment data for Sweden: averages for 5-year periods 1876–1880 (= 1880) etc. until 1940.

TABLE 7. LEVELS OF SOCIAL MOBILIZATION: SPREAD OF EDUCATION II. STUDENTS ENROLLED IN HIGHER EDUCATION AS A PRO-MILLE OF PERSONS IN AGE-GROUP 20-24 1860-1970. DENMARK, FINLAND, NORWAY, SWEDEN.

Year	Denmark	Finland	Norway[*]	Sweden[**]
1860			4.5	
1870			7.3	5.1
1880	6.3	6.7	4.7	7.7
1890	16.7	13.8	9.9	11.1
1900	19.3	17.9	8.2	8.5
1910	22.1	18.3	9.8	11.7
1920	21.1	18.4	12.3	14.8
1930	31.4	27.2	19.7	18.6
1940	37.4	31.0	21.9	26.8
1950	50.7	49.3	30.3	36.6
1960	59.2	80.5	47.6	78.4
1970	163.1	127.9	108.7	189.1

* Age-group data for Norway: average for 5-year periods 1856–1860, 1861–1865, etc. Figure for 1970: persons in age-group 20–29 divided by two.
** Enrolment data for Sweden: averages for 5-year periods 1866–1870 (= 1870), etc. until 1940.

Norway reached in the 1880s, Sweden in the 1890s and Finland as late as 1930. Jørberg (1970) interprets degree of urbanization as an indication of the countries' economic level in this period, an interpretation that is supported by the data on labour force structure and GDP per capita. Denmark passed the 50 per cent mark of labour force employed in the non-primary sector of the economy as early as in the 1880s; Norway followed in the late 1890s; Sweden just before World War I, and Finland in the 1930s. The data on GDP lead in the same direction. Furthermore, the education data seem to indicate a Danish lead over the other countries in the timing of mobilization.[23] Denmark was relatively early (in the Nordic, as well as in the European, context) in introducing a compulsory school system. Seven years of primary education was formally enacted in 1739, but was not enforced fully until after 1814 (due to poor economic conditions). Norway followed in 1827, Sweden in 1842, and Finland in 1866.[24] The data also indicate that once started, the social mobilization process accelerated most rapidly in Sweden. The differential timing of social mobilization in the Nordic countries may possibly be explained by proximity to world economic markets. Denmark has naturally had closer links with continental urban network structures in the latter half of the 19th century.

The summary table (Table 8) indicates not only a relationship between level of social mobilization and level of political participation within each country, but also a fairly good correspondence between the *ranking* of countries as to level of social mobilization and ranking of them as to level of political participation at each point in time. There is a general trend that high levels of political participation are reached before high levels of social mobilization. Although this may be an artifact of the operationalizations of levels, it is also a likely interpretation that early democratization in itself may have had mobilizing effects.

Tested on province-level. The amount of information obtainable from comparisons at the macro level is limited; especially when the number of units is as few as four. We found it also necessary to collect data on some of the core indicators of social mobilization at the level of the province in order to test relationships in a statistical manner. The independent variables focused on are urbanization, employment in the secondary sector, and employment in the secondary plus tertiary sectors, while the dependent variable remains turnout in national elections. The design has been kept as parsimonious as possible: it employs only synchronic (election by election) correlations between each of the independent variables and the dependent one. Scattergrams have likewise been run for every election in order to better judge the correlation coefficients. This

TABLE 8. SUMMARY TABLE: LEVELS OF SOCIAL MOBILIZATION AND POLITICAL PARTICIPATION

Decade	URB.	ECON. DEV. I	ECON. DEV. II	EDUC. I	EDUC. II	Ranking of countries as to overall level of social mobilization	Level of polit. part.	Un-weighted average turnout per decade	Ranking of countries as to level of political participation
1850s									
DENMARK	M		L			(1)	L	26.6	2
FINLAND	L					(2)			
NORWAY	L		L			(2)	L	30.2	1
SWEDEN	L		L			(2)			
1860s									
DENMARK	M		L			(1)	L	34.3	1
FINLAND	L					(2)			
NORWAY	L		L		L	(2)	L	28.7	2
SWEDEN	L		L			(2)			
1870s									
DENMARK	M	L	L	L	L	1	L	46.8	1
FINLAND	L	L		L	L	2			
NORWAY	L	L	L	L	L	2	L	28.6	2
SWEDEN	L	L	L	L	L	2	L	19.6	3
1880s									
DENMARK	M	L	L	L	L	1	M	60.1	1
FINLAND	L	L		L	L	3			
NORWAY	M	L	L	L	L	1	M	48.8	2
SWEDEN	L	L	L	L	L	3	L	33.3	3
1890s									
DENMARK	H	M	L	L	L	1	M	63.1	2
FINLAND	L	L		L	L	3	M		
NORWAY	M	L	L	M	L	2	M	64.8	1
SWEDEN	L	L	L	L	L	3	L	41.6	3
1900s									
DENMARK	H	M	L	L	L	1	M	63.7	2
FINLAND	L	L		L	L	4	M	66.1	1
NORWAY	M	M	L	L	L	2	M	56.4	3
SWEDEN	M	L	L	L	L	3	M	52.9	4
1910s									
DENMARK	H	M	M	M	M	1	H	74.7	1
FINLAND	L	L		L	L	4	M	60.1	3
NORWAY	M	M	L	L	L	2	M	57.7	4
SWEDEN	M	L	L	L	L	3	M	64.7	2
1920s									
DENMARK	H	H	M	M	M	1	H	77.8	1
FINLAND	L	L		L	L	4	M	56.5	4
NORWAY	M	M	M	M	L	2	M	67.8	2
SWEDEN	M	M	L	L	L	3	M	57.5	3
1930s									
DENMARK	H	H	H	M	M	1	H	80.2	1
FINLAND	H	L		L	M	4	M	63.5	4
NORWAY	M	M	M	L	L	3	H	78.9	2
SWEDEN	H	H	M	L	L	2	H	71.1	3
1940s									
DENMARK	H	H	H	H	M	1	H	86.6	1
FINLAND	M	M		L	M	4	H	76.1	3
NORWAY	M	H	H	M	M	2	H	78.6	2
SWEDEN	H	H	M	M	M	2	H	75.0	4
1950s									
DENMARK	H	H	H	H	H	1	H	81.5	1
FINLAND	H	M		M	H	4	H	76.1	4
NORWAY	H	H	H	M	M	3	H	78.5	3
SWEDEN	H	H	H	H	M	2	H	78.8	2
1960s									
DENMARK	H	H	(H)	H	H	2	H	87.0	1
FINLAND	H	H	(H)	H	H	(3)	H	84.7	3
NORWAY	H	H	(H)	H	H	(4)	H	82.5	4
SWEDEN	H	H	(H)	H	H	1	H	86.7	2

was very important in the case of Finland where the number of units has varied between only 8 and 12 *(län)*. One should of course be extremely careful in pushing interpretations too far with such a limited number of units.

The correlations for Finland (Table 9) show some clear relationships in the expected direction: urbanization and employment in the secondary sector especially seem to carry some explanatory power. But as is seen, the strong relationships decrease over time down to zero-correlations in 1958. Two factors could explain this: either that the whole country had become socially mobilized, or that the whole country had become politically mobilized. The results could mean that differences in any of the variables had become insignificant. A check of the scatterplots revealed that by the middle of the 1950s no systematic regional differences in political mobilization prevailed, except for the fact that the Åland Islands lagged enormously behind the other provinces. In 1958, for example, the range in turnout between the province with the highest turnout and the province with the lowest (disregarding Åland) was between 73 and 79 per cent. In the 1927 election there was an even and greater spread both in political participation levels and levels of employment in the secondary sector. But one noticed also a substantial spread in urbanization levels in 1958, though the levels are much higher for all provinces than 30 years earlier. The comparison of these results lead to the question: are there certain minimum levels of urbanization or economic development that have to be reached in order to produce political mobilization? An important intervening variable would probably be the penetration of parties or politicization; that is the extension and growth of local branches of nationally organized parties.

The Norwegian data (Table 10) also show clear relationships between the two indicators of economic structure (= modernization) and electoral turnout. In contrast to Finland, these relationships are consistent and stable during the whole period under study. Both social mobilization and political participation have reached all provinces, but in the Norwegian context, the *spread* on the indicators of social mobilization still accounts for the spread in electoral turnout levels. In the Finnish case, the range between the lowest and highest turnout level decreased over time.

While employment in the secondary sector correlated best with electoral turnout in Finland and Norway, urbanization is the most satisfactory variable in explaining variances in turnout in Sweden (see Table 11). The overall impression is that the indicators of economic development do not carry any decisive weight, though all correlations are positive, except for the one in 1958. The results lead to a contemplation of which explanatory variables must be sought. Why are there these

TABLE 9. FINLAND: PROVINCE LEVEL: PEARSON'S CORRELATIONS*

Election year	Urbanization and electoral turnout	Labour force in secondary sector and electoral turnout	Labour force in sec. + tertiary sectors and electoral turnout	No. of cases (*län*)
1907**				
1908	0.55	0.65	0.63	8
1909	0.43	0.54	0.51	8
1910	0.23	0.18	0.21	8
1911	0.53	0.67	0.66	8
1913	0.63	0.72	0.69	8
1916	0.57	0.59	0.53	8
1917	0.67	0.85	0.74	8
1919	0.49	0.67	0.34	9
1922	0.49	0.72	0.38	9
1924	0.55	0.79	0.47	9
1927	0.74	0.90	0.77	9
1929	0.39	0.79	0.41	9
1930**				
1933**				
1936	0.65	0.38	0.19	9
1939	0.42	0.24	0.44	10
1945	0.57	0.70	0.43	10
1948	0.33	0.53	0.17	10
1951	0.35	0.52	0.18	10
1954	0.27	0.44	0.09	10
1958	− 0.01	0.35	− 0.03	10
1962	0.18	0.58	0.23	12

* In this table, as well as Tables 10 and 11, urbanization means "% of total population living in towns"; while the labour force variables are proportions of total labour force in each case. Election data are correlated with nearest census year data.
** Missing data.

differences in importance of the few independent variables in the three different national contexts?:

	Finland	Norway	Sweden
Urbanization	Relatively important	Least important*	Most important
Employment in secondary sector	Most important	Most important	Insignificant, or no importance
Employment in secondary and tertiary sector	Least important	Relatively important	Relatively important

*See note to Table 10 to explain poor correlations

TABLE 10. NORWAY: PROVINCE LEVEL: PEARSON'S CORRELATIONS[*]

Election year	Urbanization and electoral turnout[**]		Labour force in secondary sector and turnout	Labour force in sec. + tertiary sectors and turnout	No. of cases (*Fylker*)
1888	0.07	− 0.10	0.37	0.22	20
1891	0.13	− 0.02	0.50	0.35	20
1894	0.25	0.21	0.50	0.38	20
1897	0.33	0.39	0.42	0.38	20
1900	0.38	0.28	0.43	0.42	20
1903	0.45	0.25	0.62	0.58	20
1906	0.30	− 0.20	0.40	0.40	20
1909	0.41	0.18	0.53	0.53	20
1912	0.28	0.05	0.50	0.44	20
1915	0.24	− 0.14	0.51	0.50	20
1918	0.26	− 0.22	0.46	0.48	20
1921	0.54	− 0.01	0.53	0.58	20
1924	0.50	− 0.17	0.47	0.57	20
1927	0.43	− 0.09	0.60	0.58	20
1930	0.38	0.15	0.60	0.51	20
1933	0.42	0.15	0.55	0.53	20
1936	0.44	0.32	0.66	0.60	20
1945	0.36	0.23	0.59	0.52	20
1949	0.45	0.30	0.71	0.64	20
1953	0.44	0.35	0.68	0.62	20
1957	0.34	0.25	0.67	0.58	20
1961	0.30	0.21	0.68	0.58	20
1965	0.18	0.16	0.66	0.51	20

[*] See first note on Table 9.
[**] Left-hand column: the city-provinces Oslo and Bergen included. Right-hand column: the two city-provinces excluded. It should be noted that the two provinces surrounding Oslo and Bergen respectively are recorded with no urban population (or with very insignificant urban population in the case of Akershus), but do have significant suburban populations not taken into consideration in the calculations. These facts may explain some of the unexpected correlations (e.g. minus). A better indicator of densely vs. sparsely populated areas would have resulted in higher positive correlations.

Although the number of independent variables is modest, the selected ones suffice to pin-point differences in mobilization patterns in the three countries. The results indicate that nation-specific models will have to be constructed. One phenomenon, for which we have no data, but which probably is an important intervening factor, is the *communication structure* of each of the countries. Communication is here understood in its broadest meaning: for example, build-up and spread of railways; distribution of cars; scope of telephone network; post-offices; radio and TV reception; circulation of newspapers (local *and* national). The more extensive and evenly spread these communication facilities and items, the

TABLE 11. SWEDEN: PROVINCE LEVEL: PEARSON'S CORRELATIONS[*]

Election year	Urbanization[**] and turnout		Labour force in secondary sector and turnout	Labour force in sec. + tertiary sectors and turnout	No. of cases (*län*)
1911	0.34	0.25	0.28	0.21	25
1914a	0.50	0.38	0.02	0.15	25
1914b	0.60	0.40	0.29	0.40	25
1917	0.52	0.24		0.31	25
1920	0.62	0.26		0.40	25
1921[***]					
1924[***]					
1928	0.41	0.34		0.20	25
1932	0.41	0.36		0.16	25
1936	0.33	0.35	0.10	0.16	25
1940	0.57	0.64	0.37	0.46	25
1944	0.44	0.47	0.24	0.33	25
1948	0.52	0.57	0.26	0.33	25
1952	0.51	0.56	0.17	0.35	25
1956	0.42	0.49	0.17	0.22	25
1958	0.14	0.22	− 0.02	0.02	25
1960	0.28	0.44	0.18	0.16	25

[*]   See first note to Table 9.
[**]   Left-hand column: Stockholm included. Right-hand column: Stockholm excluded.
[***] Missing data.

narrower the geographical and social distances between people are supposed to be, causing behavioural patterns and norms to conform throughout the territory. We might postulate that Sweden has reached a higher stage of national *integration*. Since we lack relevant data, the following hypothesis must serve as a tentative conclusion: communication structure is a core variable in explaining levels of political mobilization in different parts of a territory, and communication barriers are greater in Finland and Norway than in Sweden, thus creating more distinctive differences between "centre"-"periphery", and between "economic modernized"-"non-modernized" areas in the two countries as regards participation patterns.

These differences in importance of the various independent variables, dependent upon national context and time-period, should lead to a re-thinking of the original, general theoretical model drawn in Figure 3. That model could be elaborated and formalized in a number of ways in the form of functional equations.

Tempo of Social Mobilization vs. Spurts in Political Participation

Hypothesis 2: Spurts in political participation are dependent upon tempo of social mobilization. Spurts will occur in periods with accelerating social mobilization.

We have postulated that spurts in political participation will occur in periods with accelerating social mobilization. Histogram 1 and 2, and Tables 12-15 illustrate tempo of social mobilization, and in Table 16 we have made a checklist of decades bearing the marks of accelerating social mobilization by indicator and country. We have abstained from any effort to work out a composite index of tempo; it would be somewhat difficult to find criteria for weighing the importance of change in the various indicators.

Before turning to the presentation of the data, three precautions should be born in mind:

1. only data at the macro level of the nation are studied;

2. a great number of variables and phenomena have not been controlled for;

3. one should be careful in jumping to causal interpretations since the distance between the phenomena studied is great.

It should also be mentioned that one of the indicators — employment in the secondary and tertiary sector — may be misleading in the case of Denmark. As is seen, Denmark had no decades of accelerating growth in this sector in the period under study, 1870-1960. This may partly be explained by the fact that the labour force structure was fairly balanced from the outset, but one should also stress that the agricultural sector has always been more *market*-oriented in Denmark compared to the other three countries. Thus, employment in the primary sector may have had more *mobilizing* effects in the case of Denmark. Agriculture played quite a different role in the Danish economy; Jörberg (1970: 27) attributes to agriculture in Denmark the same role in terms of economic growth as shipping in Norway, industry in Sweden and timber products in Finland. The agricultural sector was Denmark's biggest earner of foreign currency, and income growth contributed to an increasing demand for non-agricultural products (Jörberg, 1970: 32), and to an agricultural-related industry.

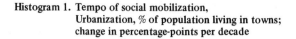

Histogram 1. Tempo of social mobilization,
Urbanization, % of population living in towns;
change in percentage-points per decade

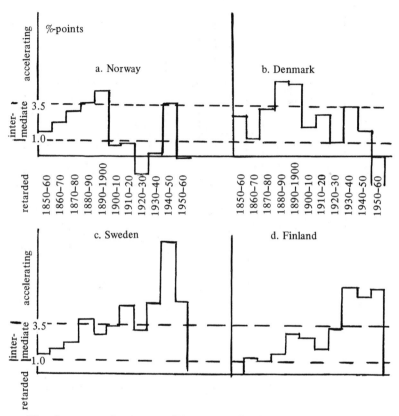

The data on urbanization (Histogram 1) show that the Danish and Norwegian development have had approximately the same structure: both countries had marked expansions of town populations in the early period. Finland and Sweden show the exact opposite pattern: a gradual development towards a more and more accelerating tempo. The peak decades in Denmark were the 1880s until the 1900s; in Norway from 1890 to 1900; and in Finland and Sweden from 1930 to 1960. The labour force data illustrate a balanced social mobilization in Denmark, without any periods of acceleration; Norway shows accelerating mobilization not only in the same decade as urbanization accelerated, 1890-1900, but also from the 1940s onwards. The growth of the industrial and service-sectors started later in Sweden, but almost like an explosion in the first decade of the

Histogram 2. Tempo of social mobilization,
% of labour force employed in the secondary
and tertiary sectors; change in percentage-points
per decade

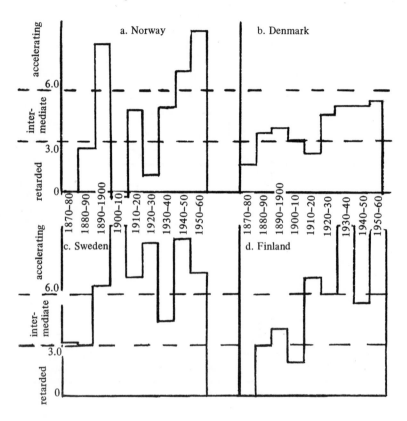

century: the proportion of the labour force employed in the secondary and tertiary sectors increased by 10 percentage-points in the ten years ![25] Finland had a similar structural-economic change in the 1930s.

The data on GDP per capita seem quite consistent with the labour force data. Again, the 1890s is seen as a period of expansion in the Norwegian economy. In Sweden both the 1890s and the 1900s indicate accelerated economic growth, but the decade with a most extraordinary growth is the 1940s, and this is also consistent with both urbanization and labour force data. Sweden was the only country virtually non-affected by the Second World War; the economies in the other countries were set back substantially, but only to grow more rapid than ever in the last five years of the decade.

The investment data are not unambiguous: the Norwegian proportions are relatively much higher than those of the other countries. All data have been taken from official statistics, but one should possibly have tried to work out what *kind* of investments. Investment rates in Norway have been "accelerating" ever since the 1890s, according to my operationalizations of tempo of economic development, while Denmark and Sweden have had an acceleration only in the last few decades. Finland has certainly shown great acceleration from the 1950s, but data have not been published for the pre-war period.[26]

It is primarily in the last two decades that there has been a so called "educational explosion": more and more young people seek (or can afford) post-elementary education at the same time as society requires educated people in order to function efficiently. Only Denmark has had earlier periods of acceleration of attendance in higher education in the 1880s and the 1920s. If the Nordic countries had been compared to other European countries, one would probably have noticed an early growth and diffusion of a primary school system: illiteracy was eliminated relatively early in a European context. And this is no insignificant point in relation to the institution of elections: large segments of the population had acquired at an early stage the skills to read and write, to influence and be influenced by others.

TABLE 12. TEMPO OF SOCIAL MOBILIZATION: GROSS INVESTMENTS IN PER CENT OF GROSS DOMESTIC PRODUCT. (DENMARK: NET NATIONAL PRODUCT). YEARLY AVERAGE PER DECADE.

(In parentheses: characterization of tempo according to scheme on p. 42)

Average for:	Denmark[*]	Finland[**]	Norway[***]	Sweden[****]
1860s			12.6 (I)	11.4 (R)
1870s	11.5 (R)		14.6 (I)	13.5 (I)
1880s	10.8 (R)		14.8 (I)	11.4 (R)
1890s	12.0 (I)		16.8 (A)	11.2 (R)
1900s	14.6 (I)		16.8 (A)	12.7 (I)
1910s	11.9 (R)		21.4 (A)	10.6 (R)
1920s	10.6 (R)		18.9 (A)	12.5 (I)
1930s	12.4 (I)		22.4 (A)	15.1 (A)
1940s	13.0 (I)		29.6 (A)	17.7 (A)
1950s	23.9 (A)	24.1 (A)	36.0 (A)	19.4 (A)
1960s	29.5 (A)	25.5 (A)	37.3 (A)	28.9 (A)

[*] 1929 prices as basis.
[**] Current prices as basis.
[***] 1860–1929: 1910 prices as basis; 1930–1949: 1938 prices as basis (figures for 1940–1945 missing); 1950–1969: 1955 prices as basis.
[****] 1861–1959: 1913-prices as basis; 1960–1969: current prices.

TABLE 13. TEMPO OF SOCIAL MOBILIZATION: % CHANGE IN GDP PER CAPITA PER DECADE.

Decades	Denmark	Norway	Sweden
1860–70			17.7 (I)
1870–80	17.4 (I)	24.1 (I)	16.1 (I)
1880–90	23.6 (I)	– 2.6 (R)	17.6 (I)
1890–00	23.1 (I)	25.6 (A)	31.8 (A)
1900–10	17.1 (I)	16.3 (I)	28.3 (A)
1910–20	10.6 (R)	22.7 (I)	23.8 (I)
1920–30	25.2 (A)	27.0 (A)	25.2 (A)
1930–40	– 3.8 (R)	22.3 (I)	22.7 (I)
1940–50	29.6 (A)	15.2 (I)	51.6 (A)

TABLE 14. TEMPO OF SOCIAL MOBILIZATION: %-POINTS CHANGE IN PROPORTIONS OF 15-19 YEAR-OLDS ATTENDING SECONDARY SCHOOLS.*

Decades	Denmark	Finland	Norway	Sweden
1870–80			0.2 (R)	
1880–90	1.0 (R)	0.9 (R)	1.8 (R)	0.2 (R)
1890–00	1.9 (R)	2.5 (R)	– 0.8 (R)	0.1 (R)
1900–10	3.9 (I)	2.9 (I)	0.2 (R)	0.8 (R)
1910–20	2.3 (I)	0.9 (R)	3.1 (I)	1.3 (R)
1920–30	3.1 (I)	5.5 (A)	– 3.4 (R)	1.2 (R)
1930–40	4.7 (I)	1.4 (R)	3.2 (I)	4.6 (I)
1940–50	10.1 (A)	14.1 (A)	4.5 (I)	18.1 (A)
1950–60	(A)	–	22.5 (A)	(A)
1960–70	(A)	–	(A)	(A)

* (A) is placed in the last cells without data: compulsory schooling was extended and changed the basis for calculating attendance in secondary schools. But in all countries there have been sharp increases in number of pupils attending *gymnasium.*

TABLE 15. TEMPO OF SOCIAL MOBILIZATION: ‰ POINTS CHANGE IN PROPORTION OF 20-24 YEAR-OLDS IN HIGHER EDUCATION

Decades	Denmark	Finland	Norway	Sweden
1860–70			2.8 (R)	
1870–80			– 2.6 (R)	2.6 (R)
1880–90	10.4 (A)	7.1 (I)	5.2 (I)	3.4 (R)
1890–00	2.6 (R)	4.1 (R)	– 1.7 (R)	– 2.6 (R)
1900–10	2.8 (R)	0.4 (R)	1.6 (R)	3.2 (R)
1910–20	– 1.0 (R)	0.1 (R)	2.5 (R)	3.1 (R)
1920–30	10.8 (A)	8.8 (I)	7.4 (I)	3.8 (R)
1930–40	6.0 (I)	3.8 (R)	2.2 (R)	8.2 (I)
1940–50	13.3 (A)	18.3 (A)	8.4 (I)	9.8 (I)
1950–60	8.5 (I)	34.2 (A)	17.3 (A)	41.8 (A)
1960–70	103.9 (A)	47.4 (A)	61.1 (A)	110.7 (A)

Examining Table 16, it seems that almost any decade since the 1890s in Sweden has been marked by some sort of accelerating social mobilization. This finding suggests, at least, that Sweden must have started on a low level, and that in terms of economic development, Denmark and Norway were ahead of Sweden before the turn of the century, and resembled each other more than either resembled Sweden's levels. The findings also indicate either that we have not been very successful in constructing a scheme of tempo of social mobilization — it has too little differentiation — or that Sweden's socio-economic development has been extraordinarily swift. The second suggestion is without doubt true (see Russett, 1964). The correctness of the first suggestion is left to others to decide. But, with little or no spread in the independent variable, there is not very much to say about relationships with a dependent one.

From Table 16 some *core* decades of accelerating social mobilization can be singled out:

Denmark: 1880s, 1920s, 1940s, 1960s
Finland: 1920s, 1940s, 1950s, 1960s
Norway: 1890s, 1920s, 1940s, 1950s, 1960s
Sweden: (1890s-1960s), most marked: 1900s, 1940s

According to Hypothesis 2, these are the decades in which to expect spurts in political participation.

As outlined in Section III, two methods of identifying spurts were proposed (using the equation of the Non-Homogeneous Diffusion Curve): (1) P = % electoral turnout; (2a) P = number of voters (= votes cast); (2b) P = number of qualified voters. In practice the methods do not lead to the same results: we have set up a comparative table that indicates which elections are identified as spurt elections by both methods, and which by only one of them. The elections that both methods identify are clearly spurts. In the cases where only one of the methods identifies spurts, method 2ab above has been chosen as the more correct, because the sum of squares of deviations are least by applying raw data. In the case of Finland, only the second method worked, the curve of percentage turnout being too irregularly shaped.

Before turning to the interpretations of the results, a note should be given on the goodness of fit of the theoretical method of curve-fitting used. As proposed in Note 15, four different equations of diffusion-curves have been applied in the runs, and from the table below comparing the squares of deviations of the values on the dependent variable, one can see that in 10 out of 11 cases, the equation argued for earlier yields the best curve-fitting. Though the fit is not astonishingly good, one may tentatively conclude that the theoretical statements on participation as a diffusion process hold some truth. But, of course, dealing with such many-sided phenomena as voting and elections, one has to leave a great deal of the variances to be explained by other variables (for example political events, socio-psychological variables, geographical distances) than by time and social mobilization.

TABLE 16. THE IDENTIFICATION OF DECADES WITH ACCELERATING
SOCIAL MOBILIZATION

Indicators	Denmark	Finland	Norway	Sweden
Urbanization.	1880s 1890s 1930s	1930s 1940s 1950s	1880s 1890s 1940s	1880s 1910s 1930s 1940s 1950s
Economic development: labour force in non-primary sectors	None	1910s 1920s 1930s 1950s	1890s 1940s 1950s	1890s 1900s 1910s 1920s 1940s 1950s
Economic development: GDP per capita	1920s 1940s	(missing data)	1890s 1920s	1890s 1900s 1920s 1940s
Economic development: gross investments	1950s 1960s	(1950s 1960s)	1890s – 1960s	1930s – 1960s
Education: secondary schools	1940s (1950s 1960s)	1920s 1940s (1950s 1960s)	1950s (1960s)	1940s (1950s 1960s)
Education: higher education	1880s 1920s 1940s 1960s	1940s 1950s 1960s	1950s 1960s	1950s 1960s

The spurt elections identified by the two methods are listed in Table 18.

What can be concluded from the results of column 1 and 3 of Table 18 about relationships between tempo of social mobilization and spurts in political participation?

In the cases of Denmark and Norway, the relationships behave more or less in the expected manner. Three of the four decades in Denmark marked by accelerating social mobilization are also accompanied by spurt elections:

Accelerating social mobilization	Spurt elections
1880s	
1920s	1920[1]-1929
1940s	1943
1960s	1966-1968

TABLE 17. COMPARISON BETWEEN FOUR DIFFERENT DIFFUSION CURVES: SUM OF SQUARES OF DEVIATIONS[*]

a Raw figures. Electorate	Gompertz	Non-Homogeneous	Modified exponential	Logistic
Denmark	5737.51	1405.19	4795.02	–
Finland	283.35	82.28	271.05	746.95
Norway	–	1201.81	9183.22	735484.88
Sweden	11810.86	1348.26	5875.96	–
b Raw figures: Votes cast				
Denmark	7261.33	1071.58	3853.34	–
Finland	1076.15	402.94	887.82	16439.26
Norway	–	613.14	7796.67	310825.83
Sweden	2035.51	630.46	2262.58	7841.50
c % Electoral turnout				
Denmark	4943.42	1664.30	2861.42	3590.49
Finland	(curve-fitting not possible)			
Norway	3724.38	2159.89	2757.62	3619.09
Sweden	1176.04	1219.38	1107.43	1329.19

[*] "–" means too large figure to be written out. The curve with the best fit has been underlined for each country.

**TABLE 18. COMPARISON OF THE TWO METHODS OF IDENTIFYING SPURTS
IN POLITICAL PARTICIPATION**

Elections	Elections identified by both methods[*]	Elections identified only when P = % turnout	Elections identified only when raw figures of electorate and votes cast are used as Ps
Denmark[**]	1853 1918 1920[2,3] 1929 1943 1966–1968	1849–1852 1866[1] 1873 1881[2]–1890 1903–1913	1920[1] 1924–1926 1932–1935
Norway	1832–1850 1885 1894–1906 1912 1921 1924	1829 1853 1882 1930–1936 1949	1909 1915–1918 1969
Sweden[**]	1887[1]–1887[2] 1911–1914[2] 1936 1948	1890–1896 1905–1908 1917 1952 1960–1968	1875–1884 1921–1932 1970
Finland			(1907) (1909) 1917–1919 (1930) 1945–1948 1966

[*]One should keep in mind that these are spurts relative to a *theoretical* model of *expected* rates of participation. Therefore the table is not directly comparable with the empirical curves of mobilization in Figure 1, p. 15. In the case of Norway, not all elections 1894–1906 are actually spurt elections, but the strong mobilization in 1894 and 1897 seems to have brought participation rates up to higher levels than were the case with pre-1894 elections. The first election in 1887 in Sweden seems to have had the same effect. Otherwise, in all elections identified in this column, there were also actual increases in the proportion of the electorates voting (compared to the rates in the immediate elections prior to the ones identified).

[**]In the case of Denmark "1920[2,3]" means "the second and third election in 1920" likewise, two elections in 1887 and in 1914 in Sweden.

Other spurt elections were 1853, 1932 and 1935. The 1930s were not a decade with marked social mobilization. The elections of the 1880s were identified as spurt elections by the method P = per cent turnout, but not by the other.

For Norway, the comparison yields this pattern:

Accelerating social mobilization	Spurt elections
1890s	1894-1897
1920s	1921-1924
1940s	
1950s	
1960s	1969

However, the elections of the 1900-1918 period were also labelled spurt elections: this is an unexpected outcome, but may be an example of a serious shortcoming of the method. During this period the electorate was twice widened considerably as results of change in suffrage rules, thus creating "shocks" in the curves of diffusion. One way of circumventing this problem could possibly be to differentiate *size* of the spurts. For example:

$$\frac{(\text{empirical no. of voters} - \text{calculated no. of voters}) \times 100}{\text{no. of qualified voters}}$$

This formula would yield spurt elections for the same years, but would offer the possibility, in an objective way, of identifying the elections with significant spurts. This control, however, is not carried out here at this stage, due to the substantial amount of calculation work involved.

The Finnish data give also a partial confirmation of the expectations:

Accelerating social mobilization	Spurt elections
1920s	
1940s	1945-1948
1950s	
1960s	1966

The elections during the fight for independence and the Civil War, 1917-1919 were also characterized as spurt elections. The data for Sweden are more difficult to interpret, both because most decades are marked by accelerating social mobilization and because spurt elections occur even before the tempo of social mobilization accelerated! One case causing "inconvenient" results is certainly sufficient for raising some critical doubts about the methods chosen. The constructed scheme of tempo of social mobilization may be misleading; the theory behind it, and the selected curve of diffusion, may be obscure; or simply just the two methods combined. On the other hand, the methods seem capable of describing the relationships in the other countries. Thus, instead of discarding any of the methods at this stage, one might rather urge further analyses to be performed with smaller units of analysis such as provinces or communes. The basic reason for not reaching any clear-cut conclusions may be found in the decision to work with data on an abstract macro-level: too large a margin is left for casual relationships. Moving a few steps down the macro-micro ladder will permit a far greater number of cases to be tested, and whatever the outcome of such analyses, the conclusions would be more final as to the applicability of the methods.

Political Participation over Time: Centre-Periphery

Hypothesis 3: The curves of political participation over time will have approximately similar shapes in the politically most central region and the geographical-politically most peripheral region of a nation, but there will be a difference in timing of the different phases. The "take-off" phase in the process of diffusion will be lagging in the periphery.

The accompanying Figures 5-7 all demonstrate that centre-periphery relations have consequences for levels of political mobilization in the Nordic countries. Except for the last few elections, which show a levelling out of differences, the centres are more mobilized than the peripheries. The shape of the curves, and the fact that the centres mobilized earlier than the peripheries, correspond to the theoretical conception drawn in Figure 4. But as is seen, although the trend over time is unambiguous, there are great irregularities in the mobilization curves. And what is striking is that the irregularities are consistent for centre and periphery; that is, the two curves seem to a very large degree to follow each other. This result leads to the following interpretation. A variable, independent of time, social mobilization, and political centrality, is in operation; that is, in a model of political mobilization one probably will have to include a variable called "political events", but how to define and operationalize this variable is more difficult. One will have to search for fundamental cleavages in the social system (for example, issues related to language, school-system, social welfare, government, defence, alliances), and locate the years in which issues related to these cleavages were prominent. One way of finding out whether certain issues have or have not played a part in an election is to look at *polarization* scores; that is, check the existence of

Figure 5. % Electoral turnout: Finland 1907-1962

"Centre" = – – – – – – – – – – (unweighted averages)

"Periphery" = ───────

Missing data: 1907, 1930, 1933.

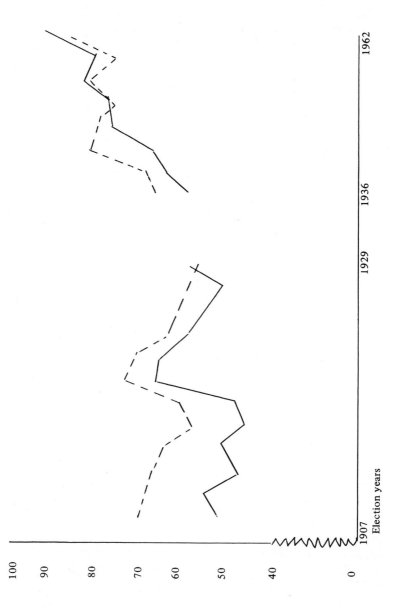

Figure 6. % Electoral turnout: Norway 1829-1969

"Centre" = – – – – – – – – – – (unweighted averages)

"Periphery" = ————————

For period 1829–1856, data only on *registered* voters, not the total number of *qualified* voters.
The curves for "centre" and "periphery" can be compared, but not the curve for "centre" (or "periphery") 1829–1856 and 1859–1969.
Data are missing for the province Troms 1829–1865.

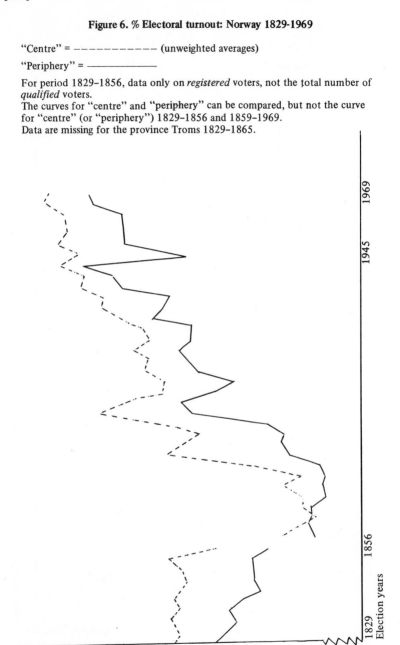

Figure 7. % Electoral turnout: Sweden 1911-1960

"Centre" = – – – – – – – – – – (unweighted averages)

"Periphery" = ─────────

Missing data: 1921, 1924.

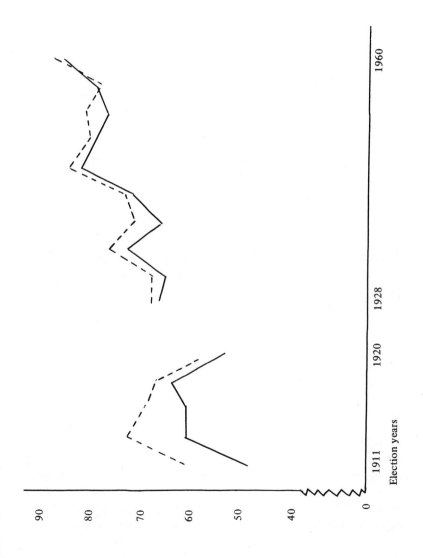

cultural polarization (for example, support for "cultural" plus "non-cultural" parties vs. support for "culturally indifferent" parties), economic polarization (for example, support for socialist parties and conservative parties vs. support for parties essentially grounded on "non-economic" issues). A hypothesis would be: the more polarization, the higher the mobilization, or the greater the probability of spurts in political participation. The question of how to evaluate the importance of size of polarization scores would have to be decided by looking at and comparing such scores for a great number of elections. A more parsimonious strategy of locating the role of "political events" would be to interpret degree of party competition as an indicator of polarization or as an indicator of the importance of issues and of political events. The expectation would be that the closer the race between two big parties or two government alternatives is expected to be (by the voters), the higher the political mobilization (see for example Svåsand, 1972: 89-102).

Again, as was the tentative conclusion reached on pp. 52-53 above, centre-periphery differences seem to be least in Sweden. The distance between the two mobilization curves is negligible from about 1920 onwards. In Finland, differences were marked in the early period, but have narrowed through time, until the last few elections the periphery has been even more mobilized than the centre. In Norway, centre-periphery differences have been most persistent throughout the entire period of election history. We choose to interpret and explain these inter-nation differences in the same way as in a previous section, by considering differences in communication barriers; that is, one might say that periphery in Norway is more "peripheral" than periphery in Sweden and Finland. This is also a way of giving the terms of "centre" and "periphery" new contents: we started out with a definition of "periphery" as being the area most distant in geographical terms from the *political* centre of the nation. In a redefinition one should take into account the number of "inter-area" links within a nation; to what extent are people in peripheral Norway knowledgeable about and involved in the activities of the political centre, compared to people in peripheral Sweden vis à vis their political centre?

A crude example of operationalization might be the proportions of the "centre" and the "periphery" populations respectively who read "national" newspapers in each of the three countries. This is one example of measuring distances or barriers of communication. Whether communication variables are vital in the definition of "centre"-"periphery", and whether these considerations are valid in explaining the differences in the Nordic context, remains to be seen.

V. CONCLUSION

Some core variables explaining increasing political participation have been located – different indicators of social mobilization and emergence of mass parties. A theoretical model of assumed interrelationships was proposed but we have not been able so far to construct a strict unified model that can be tested empirically; that is, a model that possesses the characteristics of being verifiable. We can only conclude in *general* terms that there are certain relationships between: (1) level of social mobilization and political participation; (2) tempo of social mobilization and spurts in political participation; (3) institutional heritage and patterns of initial political mobilization; (4) organization, presence of mass parties and political participation; (5) political/geographical location and political participation.

However, the relationships and interrelationships are ambiguous and much more complex than this piece of work has been able to demonstrate. In *specific* terms it can be concluded that some distinct differences between Finland, Norway and Sweden were identified with the help of provincial data. Differences in levels of political participation could be attributed to a larger degree to differences in economic structure in Finland and Norway than in Sweden, and centre-periphery differences are more prevalent in Finland and Norway. One way of explaining this was suggested: to collect and analyse information on degrees of national integration and communication structures in the three countries.

How to interpret the meaning of political participation? *One* interpretation that we find essential, is to regard voting as a kind of *pressure* upon the socio-political system. We have been pre-occupied only with the "input"-side of the box called "the political system", but what goes on within the box and what comes out of it is dependent upon what is fed in. We have focused upon one aspect of this feeding-in process: variations in levels of participation. The next step is to analyse in detail what goes into the box – e.g., which parties compete, and what representatives are elected – and to study the consequences for decision-making procedures and policy-outcomes. Voting is an act that demands a reaction, or a *response* from the political system. The number of votes, and the composition of votes, are to some extent a consequence of this response in the next round.

In periods of rapid social mobilization the pressure upon the political system is thought to be more intense than otherwise. What happens when societies have reached overall high levels of social mobilization (like the Nordic countries of today)?

Some of the indicators of social mobilization are also indicators of collective and individual resource accumulation (e.g., GDP per capita, higher education). As resources accumulate, with society becoming wealthier, one hypothesis could be that the question of who is to decide upon the applications and distributions of the resources grows more important and stimulates steady high levels of participation.

But another hypothesis is just as likely: when society (and its individuals) becomes "rich" people tend to be more indifferent to the question of who governs.

Which of the two hypotheses is the most likely is possibly highly interrelated with the (equal/unequal) distribution of resources and the proportions of resources available for disposal for public and private goods respectively. The scope of public activity and public goods has increased considerably in the Nordic countries during the post-World War II period. These goods are mainly the result of demands channelled through the institutions of elections, parties and organizations of various kinds. An important question is: at what stage (if any) will the demand be that such and such parts of one's income should be reserved for private goods? (In the early 1970s, the public sector consumed about 50 per cent of national income).

What we have in mind is that the modernization process, or social mobilization, has generated a complete new area of political conflict in Western mixed-economy democracies. Who shall have the privilege to decide upon how an increasing value accumulation in society ought to be consumed (e.g., the "State", representative assemblies, or the individual citizen)? The theme of conflict is "new" in the sense that the share of the public sector of the national product has never before in history been as large as now, and the share has risen *rapidly* the last 30-40 years. Is it likely that Western democracies will maintain a *mixed*-economy in the long run? If not, what are the implications for "democracy"? These questions shall not be answered here. Nor shall we here engage in a discussion of what is "democracy". The purpose is to launch the hypothesis that these will be lasting, recurring themes of conflict, perhaps *the* crucial ones, for many years to come, and that they will contribute to the maintenance of the high levels of political mobilization that the countries have achieved.

But these are speculations valid only for these systems, with *their* organization of (economic and) political institutions. A relevant question is: if rapid social mobilization and a high level of social mobilization create a strong and constant pressure on the political system, what will be the political consequences in countries *lacking* institutions of participation (elections, parties, representative organs) and undergoing accelerating social mobilization? Bearing in mind the danger of measuring performance in other societies with the standards of our own (and perhaps neglecting other forms of institutions of participation), we will hypothesize that societies with such characteristics will experience a greater number of open political conflicts (measured by number of demonstrations, strikes, degree of corruption, changes of cabinets, turnover in cabinet positions, *coups d'état*). Our belief is that societies lacking a fundamental institution of participation that allows secret (i.e., free from social pressure) voting will be more unstable than societies having such an institution.

Notes

1. By "political incorporation" is meant the extension of suffrage to larger and larger groups of the population. The concept can also refer to the degree of power allocated to popular-elected assemblies, or the changes of different elected groups of participation in a government coalition. (See for example Stinchcombe, 1968: 173-175.)

2. These nations are considered "comparable". For a discussion of what cases to select for comparison, see Lijphart (1973). Smelser (1967: 111-113) has identified the *problem* with which the comparative analyst has to deal as "data which cannot be controlled experimentally and the number of cases of which is too small to permit statistical analysis", and he further states that the proper *method* is to investigate comparable national or inter-nation cases: "The more similar two or more [cases] are with respect to crucial variables . . . the better able is the investigator to isolate and analyze the influence of other variables that might account for the differences he wishes to explain." The "crucial" variables in this study are geographical setting and general historical-political development. The development of political incorporation has been fairly similar in at least three of the countries, thus enabling us to hold one aspect of the institutional setting constant − an aspect that is "crucial" with respect to the dependent variable. However, we shall draft the inter-nation differences that exist, and discuss the possible effect of these, see below.

3. In his article in *APSR* (1961), Deutsch presented data for these selected indices of social mobilization: GNP, GNP per capita, total population, radio audience, newspaper readers, literates, work-force in non-agricultural occupations, urban population. Lerner (1958) used data on urbanization, mass media development and literacy, while Flora (1973) focused on urbanization and education data.

4. It should be stressed that the indicators selected are to be understood in the light of the historical periods under study: we may have to look for other indicators of both social mobilization and political participation in a study of the Nordic countries, say in the year A.D. 2000.

5. Instead of specifying references for every historical fact outlined in the text, I list the authors consulted in the composition of this section: Andrén (1965), Bull (1926), Hadenius (1968), Holmberg (1969), Hornberg (1948), Høgh (1972), Lipset and Rokkan (1967), Pesonen (1969), *Problemer i Nordisk historieforskning* (1967), Puntila (1964), Rokkan and Meyriat (1969), Rokkan (1970), Törnudd (1968), Verney (1957), Wallin (1961), Winding (1967).

6. For an overview of election procedures, see Rokkan and Meyriat (1969).

7. But not the most democratic system as some Danish historians claim, see Marstrand et al. (1929: 42). France, Greece, Prussia and several Swiss cantons had all introduced more comprehensive systems (cf. Rokkan and Meyriat, 1969).

8. "Astronomical time" is the expression of Sorokin and Merton (1937). They distinguish this concept of time from the concept of "social time", which expresses the "change or movement of social phenomena in terms of other· social phenomena taken as points of reference".

9. Due to space consideration the graphs had to be left out in this account.

10. Of course, "reality" does not fit into a closed system of arrows and boxes. Increase in participation may in its turn result in an increase in educational opportunities and educational levels. Relationships are interdependent, and we should be aware of feedback-processes. Important institutions and facts of social and political life have also been left out in this simplistic conception.

11. The idea of this model, though here applied in a somewhat different form and for another purpose, must be credited Aarebrot and Rokkan (1971: 24).

12. See Rose and Urwin (1971) for a more detailed discussion of the spatial and status dimensions of differentiation in social structure.

13. The model to be applied assumes personal (direct) communication, but it is impossible to exclude the possibility of indirect communication (e.g., through newspapers). In most diffusion studies it is difficult to differentiate the two sources of influence: person-to-person or mass media.

14. Hernes (1972: 175).

15. Estimations of the parameters for the Non-Homogeneous Diffusion curve, see Hernes (1972). A computer programme that calculates the theoretical values has been made by Jarle Brosveet and Helge Østbye (of the Institute of Sociology, Bergen), and will be applied here. Their programme also makes possible a comparison with other models: the Gompertz equation, the modified exponential, and the logistic curve. The estimations of the parameters for these curves have been based on the procedures followed by Croxton et al. (1967: 262-280).

16. Myklebost (1960) has collected data on the development of agglomerations in Norway from 1875. But similar collections are not available for the other countries. It is also questionable what his definition of an agglomeration (among other things that it must have at least 200 inhabitants, and the distances between dwellings must not exceed 50 metres) really implies.

17. Another frequently used indicator of population concentration – persons per km^2 – could have been applied, but is not considered fruitful in a Nordic context with large mountain areas in Norway and great number of lakes in Finland.

18. Hage (1973: 5) is concerned with similar problems. He poses questions like "What does it mean to say slow, medium or fast rates of change; *Future shock* is a household word but what is its reality in societal analysis? How does one combine in equations variables that change at different rates?" Hage does not offer any *a priori* answers to his questions.

19. Russett (1964: 54): Percentage of population in cities over 20,000. It should be noted that Russett's tables of this kind are unclear, and have to be read carefully. The title above the data entries reads: "average annual % increase". What he means is "average annual increase in %-points", for his formula, (50), states that "the average annual increase in Table 10 is simply the percentage in the later year, minus the percentage in the earlier year, with the remainder divided by the number of years elapsed".

20. Rostow (1960) used National Income as basis instead of GDP.

21. Mostly annual averages for the years 1950-1959.

22. "province" = *län* and *fylke*. Denmark is excluded due the considerable amount of work involved in arranging and coding the electoral results of the pre-1920 period.

23. The data on enrolment in secondary schools are not easily comparable (see note below Table 6). But the data on enrolment in higher education are more reliable in a comparative perspective.

24. But these "formal" years say nothing about the actual build-up of schools, and the efficiency of the systems. In Finland, e.g., as late as in 1891, nearly 50 per cent of the children in primary schools received their education only one day a week, or in their families (Levasseur, 1897: 224).

25. Lafferty (1971: 42-77) has carried out detailed comparisons of economic development in Denmark, Norway and Sweden in the period 1870-1930/40. The general conclusions reached here are highly compatible with his, though his analysis of industrial surges on the basis of investment data shows different patterns. This is partly due to different strategies of analysis, and partly due to the choice of a *time unit*. Lafferty has used *5-year periods* as units where I have used *decades*. Thus, there may exist a "temporal fallacy" of the same character as the ecological fallacy. For a discussion of this point, see paper by Odén (1973).

26. Early data on the other countries are all results of recent research on national accounts and national products.

References

AAREBROT, FRANK, H. and STEIN ROKKAN (1971) "Nation-Building, Democratization, and Mass Mobilization: Initial Results of a Statistical Analysis of Norwegian Data." University of Bergen (mimeo).

ANDRÉN, NILS (1965) Nordisk statskunskap. Stockholm: Liber.

BULL, EDVARD (1926) Grunnriss av Norges historie. Oslo: Aschehoug.

CIPOLLA, CARLO M. (1969) Literacy and Development in the West. London: Penguin.

CLARK, COLIN (1951) Conditions of Economic Progress. London: 2nd ed.

CROXTON, F. D., D. J. COWDEN and S. KLEIN (1967) Applied General Statistics. Englewood Cliffs, N.J.: Prentice Hall.

DEUTSCH, KARL W. (1961) "Social Mobilization and Political Development." *American Political Science Review,* 55: 493-514.

FLORA, PETER (1973) Modernisierungsforschung: Zur empirischen Analyse der gesellschaftlichen Entwicklung. Bd. I.: Model, Methoden, Analysen. konstanz: dissertation, University of Konstanz (January, mimeo).

GALTUNG, JOHAN (1971) Members of Two Worlds: A study of Three Villages in Western Sicily. Oslo: U-forlaget.

HADENIUS, STIG (1968) Sverige efter 1900. Stockholm: Aldus/Bonniers.

HAGE, JERALD (1973) "Theoretical Decision Rules for Research Design and Data Collection." Paper presented at the ISSC-Seminar on "Macro-Contexts and Micro-Variations in Cross-National Research". Helsinki (September).

HERNES, GUDMUND (1972) "The Process of Entry into First Marriage." *American Sociological Review,* 37 (April).

HIRSCHMAN, ALBERT O. (1970) Exit, Voice and Loyalty. Cambridge, Mass.: Harvard University Press.

HOLMBERG, ÅKE (1969) Sverige efter 1809. Verdandis skriftserie 9. Stockholm: Svenska Bokförlagen.

HORNBERG, EIRIK (1948) Finlands historia från eldsta tid till våra dager. Malmö: Allhems fölag.

HØGH, ERIK (1972) Vaelgeradfaerd i Danmark 1849-1901: en politisk og sociologisk analyse. Copenhagen: J. Paludans forlag.

JÖRBERG, LENNART (1970) The Industrial Revolution in Scandinavia 1850-1914. London: Collins. IV, Chapter 8 in the series: The Fontana Economic History of Europe, which is being edited by CARLO M. CIPOLLA.

KUHNLE, STEIN (1972) "Stemmeretten i 1814: beregninger over antall stemmerettskvalifiserte etter Grunnloven." Historisk Tidsskrift, 51, no. 4: 373-391.

LAFFERTY, WILLIAM (1971) Economic Development and the Response of Labor in Scandinavia, Oslo: U-forlaget.

LAMPARD, ERIC E. (1965) "Historical Aspects of Urbanization" in P. M. HAUSER and C. F. SCHNORE (eds.), The Study of Urbanization. New York.

LAPALOMBARA, JOSEPH and MYRON WEINER (eds.) (1966) "The Origin and Development of Political Parties" in Political Parties and Political Development. Princeton: Princeton University Press.

LERNER, DANIEL (1958) The Passing of Traditional Society: Modernizing the Middle East. New York: The Free Press.

LEVASSEUR, E. (1897) L'enseignement primaire dans les pays civilisés. Paris.

LIJPHART, AREND (1973) "Comparative Analysis: The Search for Comparable Cases." Paper presented at the ISSC-seminar on "Macro-Contexts and Micro-Variations in Cross-National Research." Helsinki (September).

LIPSET, SEYMOUR M. and STEIN ROKKAN (eds.) (1967) Party Systems and Voter Alignments. New York: The Free Press.

MARSTRAND, E., A. BOJE, and F. SÖRENSEN (1929) Den Danske Stat. Copenhagen: Martins Forlag.

MULHALL, M. G. (1884) The Dictionary of Statistics. London.

MYKLEBOST, HALLSTEIN (1960) Norges tettbygde steder 1875-1950. Oslo: U-forlaget.

NOUSIAINEN, JAAKKO (1966) Finlands politiska system. Stockholm: Svenska Bokförlaget.

ODÉN, BIRGITTA (1973) "On Aggregation of Time." Paper presented at the ISSC-seminar on "Macro-Contexts and Micro-Variations in Cross-National Research." Helsinki (September).

PESONEN, PERTTI (1969) "Political Parties and the Finnish Eduskunta: Voters' Perspectives, Party Nominations, and Legislative Behaviour." University of Tampere and University of Iowa (mimeo).

Problemer i Nordisk historieforskning: Fremveksten av de politiske partier på 1800-tallet(1967). Bergen: U-forlaget.

PUNTILA, L. (1964) Finlands politiska historie 1809-1955. Helsingfors: Svenska Bokförlaget.

ROKKAN, STEIN and JEAN MEYRIAT (1969) International Guide to Electoral Statistics. The Hague-Paris: Mouton.

ROKKAN, STEIN (1970) Citizens, Elections, Parties. New York: McKay.

ROSE, RICHARD and DEREK URWIN (1971) "Territorial Differentiation and Political Unity in Western Nations: A Preliminary Analysis." Paper presented to the ISSC/ECPR Workshop on Indicators of National Development: Lausanne.

ROSTOW, W. W. (1960) The Stages of Economic Growth. Cambridge: The University Press.

RUSSETT, BRUCE M., HAYWARD R. ALKER, KARL W. DEUTSCH, and HAROLD LASSWELL (1964) World Handbook of Political and Social Indicators. New Haven: Yale University Press.

SANDVEN, JOHANNES and ANNA-LIISA SYSIHARJU (eds.) (1966) Veien til og gjennom gymnaset i de nordiske land. Oslo: U-forlaget.

SMELSER, NEIL J. (1967) "Notes on the methodology of Comparative Analysis of Economic Activity." *Transactions of the Sixth World Congress of Sociology.* 2. Evian, International Sociological Association.

SOROKIN, PITIRIM A. and ROBERT K. MERTON (1937) "Social Time: A Methodological and Functional Analysis." *The American Journal of Sociology,* **XLII,** (March): 615-689.

STINCHCOMBE, ARTHUR L. (1968) Constructing Social Theories. New York: Harcourt, Brace & World Inc.

SVÅSAND, LARS G. (1972) "Stortingsvalget i 1882: en analyse av geografiske og økonomiske konflikter," Institute of Sociology, Bergen (mimeo).

TÖRNUDD, KLAUS (1968) The Electoral System of Finland. London: Hugh Evelyn.

VERNEY, DOUGLAS V. (1957) Parliamentary Reform in Sweden 1866-1921. Oxford: The Clarendon Press.

WALLIN, GUNNAR (1961) Valrörelser och valresultat: Andra-kammarvalen i Sverige 1866-1884. Stockholm: Ronzo Boktryckeri AB.

WINDING, KJELL (1967) Danmarks Historie. Denmark: Fremads Fokusbpöger.

ØSTBYE, HELGE (1972) "Om innföring av fjernsyn i Norge". Sekretariatet for mediaforskning, Institute of Sociology, Bergen (mimeo).

Stein Kuhnle is a research Associate at the Institute of Sociology at the University of Bergen, from which he received his cand. polit. degree in politics in 1973.